W9-BSU-497

Adult Learners in the Academy

Adult Learners in the Academy

Lee Bash
Baldwin-Wallace College

Anker Publishing Company, Inc.
Bolton, Massachusetts

Adult Learners in the Academy

ISBN 1-882982-60-6

Composition by Deerfoot Studios
Cover design by Frederick Schneider/Grafis

Anker Publishing Company, Inc.
176 Ballville Road
P.O. Box 249
Bolton, MA 01740-0249 USA

www.ankerpub.com

About the Author

Lee Bash has been dean of the Division of Lifelong Learning at Baldwin-Wallace College (B-W) since 1999. Dr. Bash received his PhD at SUNY-Buffalo. His more than 30 years in adult, college, and high school education have taken him from teacher, professor, and administrator to researcher, author, lecturer, and consultant. His busy life included ten years in Kentucky where he served as chair of Fine and Performing Arts at Bellarmine College while concurrently holding the post of director of the Kentucky Governor's School of the Arts.

He has published five books and more than 200 articles during his career. In recent years, Dr. Bash has been in great demand as he has presented his research and papers for numerous organizations devoted to the adult learner. His regular column, "Bash on Books," was featured for more than 15 years in *Jazz Educators Journal.* He continues to write articles occasionally for *Jazziz Magazine.*

In 2000, Dr. Bash completed the prestigious Management and Leadership in Education program at Harvard University. In 2001, he led a team of faculty from B-W at the American Association of Colleges and Universities (AAC&U) titled "Sustaining Innovative Leadership on the Campus." Dr. Bash has also contributed a chapter to *The Administrative Portfolio,* edited by Peter Seldin and Mary Lou Higgerson (Anker, 2002).

Table of Contents

Preface

Although it may not be immediately apparent, phenomena associated with adult learner programs and the 21st century academy are powerfully and inextricably linked. This book is designed to assist any faculty member or administrator who wants to understand how the impact of adult learning programs has already helped transform the academy and how newer initiatives are likely to impact their own campus in the coming decades. I can think of no more challenging and exhilarating place to be than in the academy as it undergoes what I believe is the most exciting transformation in its many centuries of existence. The premise of this book is based on the notion that adult learning programs are at the forefront of the change that higher education is experiencing (indeed, some believe they are leading the parade!). In most cases, institutions of higher learning, regardless of their formal involvement with adult learning, are probably utilizing strategies and activities that are direct byproducts of benchmark adult learner programs, though they may not be aware of the source. Furthermore, the adult learner is a ubiquitous part of this century's educational landscape, comprising almost 50% of all students enrolled.

The purpose of this book is to serve as a wake-up call for those members of the academy who may have a preference to work primarily with traditional students. Adult learning programs have already made a surprising impact, especially via technology, an emphasis on learning-centered activities, and other exciting initiatives that have helped redefine common practice on the campus. Their influence is likely to expand significantly. So even if you don't ever expect to work directly with adult learner programs, understanding their influence on all parts of the academy in the midst of the sea change higher learning is currently experiencing should help you achieve a more holistic understanding of steps any institution may wish to take to flourish in this highly charged change environment.

While there is a growing body of literature concerning the adult learner, it is almost exclusively devoted to the theoretical, analytical, and critical aspects of the domain. And yet, when I talk with my colleagues who share common leadership roles in the adult learning community, our conversation inevitably focuses on the human-interest stories that predominate the field. For instance, it is when I hear about an adult learner who tells her husband she is in a bowling league on Tuesday nights for six years after he forbids her to go to college that I fully understand the power and multiple-layered implications of what adult learners are likely to face in the pursuit of higher education. It is during these times that our passions are clearly evident and it is during these exchanges that I always feel most excited about the future of higher education.

This book is intended to capture some of those insights through the extensive use of case studies. By blending some of the theoretical aspects of adult learning with many of the practical and personal components that characterize higher learning in the 21st century, I have tried to capture something special for the reader to enjoy in this book.

And finally, I prefer to frame much of the learning I envision on the campus of the future under the domain of "lifelong learning" in its most literal application: where the college or university campus serves as the learning resource and center for learners of all ages—from cradle to grave—and meets all types of needs—from formal to the most casual learning expectation. It is this very model upon which this book is based and the vision that defines and impels my work and enthusiasm.

Outline of the Book

Part One: Context and Overview, is designed to examine adult learning from four perspectives: adult programs, adult learners, demographics and projections, and programmatic best practices. Part One strives to establish a foundation upon which the remainder of the book is built. In many ways, it was created with a broader brush to help provide an overview and big picture perspective in the hope that once the reader understands these concepts, he or she will be able to generalize them throughout the remainder of the book.

Part Two: Where Adult Learners Begin Their Educational Journey, marks one of the most notable distinctions between adult learners and their younger classmates. Adult learners face special challenges such as fitting learning into an already busy schedule, pursuing studies when their responsibilities are already likely to be overextended, and placing themselves into an environment they often perceive as hostile and frightening.

These topics, as well as some of the motivations and impulses that contribute to their decision to continue their education in the first place, are covered within this section. It also looks at why adult learners seek college-level learning and what they bring with them to the academy, and examines a largely overlooked population that will be the fastest growing and quite possibly the most powerful demographic: senior citizens as learners.

Part Three examines institutional responses to the adult learner. Whereas the previous section looks at adult learner programs from the student's perspective, Part Three addresses programmatic perspectives and the fundamental needs required to sustain these programs. Three chapters comprise this section: what adults need in their learning environment, the problem of disconnection between the adult learner and institutions whose primary focus may be on the traditional student, and the importance of entrepreneurialism in preparing the academy for the 21st century.

Finally, Part Four reminds the reader that education is no longer an end game. The single chapter in this section looks at some meaningful applications of the term "lifelong learning" as well as some projections regarding how the 21st century academy is likely to change.

Lee Bash
August 2002

Acknowledgments

I am humbled by the amount of assistance I have received in preparation for this book. Many people lent their skills and support in a manner I can never repay. But at least I can share my heartfelt appreciation to the many wonderful people who gave freely and tirelessly in their support of this project.

To begin, I offer special gratitude to Kristin Lighty who spent countless hours talking with me about these ideas in their formative stages many years ago. Despite the daily life-threatening challenges Kristin now faces, her spirit always serves to inspire me. Kristin, I wrote every page with you in mind.

I want to say a special thank-you to every one of the hundreds of adult learners I have encountered in the past. A small piece of each of you is contained in the case studies, since each is a composite (though a few of you have contributed details, inspiration, and attitudes that sparked the germinal impulse). I also want to offer sincere thanks to Mary Lou Higgerson for her support and encouragement of this project in the first place. She continues to inspire me in all tasks I encounter. Many folks contributed in the day-to-day details and operations that moved this project along. Eleanor Nolan, Shirley Ashton, Winnie Gerhardt, Amy Hershiser, Mary Ann Leibold, Margie Martyn, Judie May, Ria Solloway, and Anna Hogan: you can't imagine how much you have helped me in the myriad of tasks you perform. But I have especially come to rely on Sue Grunau for her careful editing of the manuscript, her far-ranging knowledge of the subject matter, and her willingness to challenge every word I have written. If there are any good ideas or passages contained in these pages, they are probably due to her influence and help.

Finally, I offer my undying appreciation to my wife, Sandy, who provided daily support and encouragement, as well as careful proofreading and assistance. She is a partner in the full sense of the word.

Acknowledgments

PART ONE

CONTEXT AND OVERVIEW

1

Adult Programs: Why They Are Important to the 21st Century College or University

Overview

Although adult learning programs have grown significantly on the majority of campuses in the US during the past 20 years, these programs are seldom fully integrated into the mainstream of the institution by either faculty or administration. Typically, the initial impulse to include adult learners as a portion of the school's population is likely to be predicated on purely bottom line considerations. As a result, while many schools may increase their profit margins by targeting and pursuing adult learners, they are likely to eventually encounter a wide-ranging set of problems unless they address those philosophical, pedagogical (andragogical), and foundational aspects of adult learning that comprise best practices.

As the academy enters the 21st century, certain market realities have forced most colleges and universities to rethink their priorities and mission. Among dramatic new demographics that include the "graying of America," a level of competition among schools that approaches cutthroat aspects more common in business practice, technological advances moving at light speed, and slimmer operational margins, many schools are facing challenges that threaten their very existence. Consequently, the academy is being asked to redefine itself in order to survive and thrive in the new century. One of the central strategies being employed by many institutions is the meaningful integration of adult programs to support what has become a significant portion of the student population.

The challenge for these schools is to create programs of substance rather than superficial facades since the ability to sustain such programs will be critical. While many on the campus may question the need for a dynamic adult program, there is ample evidence of the benefits that can be obtained with such a strategy. This chapter examines the "so what?" question regarding the need for meaningful integration of adult learners into the full fabric of the 21st century academy.

INTRODUCTION

Higher education in America today is almost certainly at its pinnacle as we step into the 21st century. As such, it reflects a century that has achieved greater access for more students, regardless of their income and social class than ever before, bundled by a transformation in thinking that has moved from education as end game to lifelong learning as a guiding principle. One of the foremost aspects of higher education in the 21st century is the growing importance of the adult learner, even as the academy seeks avenues to retain its sense of purpose and function within the narrower perspective of the traditional student. As noted by Canja (2002):

> Perhaps no area of lifecycle perception has been so transformed and is so transforming as the concept of learning. No longer can it be relegated to the young. The importance of lifelong learning has grown exponentially. According to the National Center for Education Statistics, 90 million Americans participated in some kind of formal adult learning in 1999. (p. 27)

Canja placed these comments into a more meaningful perspective when she observed:

> First, lifelong learning has become an economic necessity for national and global productivity. With the decline in birth rates in major developed countries, it is older persons—still active, still healthy—who must continue in the workforce, trained and retrained. (p. 27)

However, Lovett (2002) recognized that the extensive challenges posed by this new population have seldom been recognized when she asserted that:

> Another threat to higher education's foundation emerged in the 1980's, but went unnoticed, at least initially. The threat

> came from the reluctance of traditional colleges and universities, both public and private, to accommodate the needs and preferences of new, nontraditional participants in higher education. The prosperity of the 1990s masked the depth and breadth of this problem. Well-employed adult students, or in some cases their employers, stepped into the gap and chose to pay relatively high tuition to new institutions able to provide good instruction and mentoring, along with convenient schedules. (p. 12)

Prior to investigating institutional challenges, let us begin by examining those special issues that face programs that deal explicitly with the adult learner.

Problems Facing Adult Learning Programs

Low Status

Adult programs often suffer from low status on their own campus. Although some forms of adult learning programs can be traced all the way back to land grant initiatives in the middle of the 19th century, most faculty and administrators probably relate to the more recent, post–World War II efforts when thinking about this topic. Adult education has drawn heavily on a pre-professional orientation and curricular track that has often been viewed by faculty and administrators as being too marginal and not mainstream enough when compared to the services and support offered full-time students between the ages of 18 and 22 (Sissel, Hansman, & Kasworm, 2001). The consequences of these attitudes and actions can be profound:

> This fixation on youth is particularly autocratic given that historically, two of the hallmarks of higher education policy in the United States centered around the learning needs of adults: the enactment of the Morrill Act's creation of land grant universities in 1862 and the GI Bill in 1944. Thus, although new federal legislation may be essential to making change, policymaking alone cannot, and will not, be the sole mechanism by which the youth-oriented hegemonic structure of U.S. higher education will be recreated into a system that meets the needs of learners of all ages. (p. 21)

As a consequence, adult-centered learning programs on many campuses may be looked upon with suspicion or disdain among faculty members and administrators. These constituents often appear to assume that the objective (or at least, covert objective) of adult programs is to dilute the curriculum and reduce the credibility of the institution. Typically, the adult programs tend to be tolerated among their detractors more for the revenues they are likely to generate than for any other reason. Furthermore, as a reflection of how marginalized these programs may become, faculty members will often either abrogate their teaching responsibilities entirely when it comes to adult learners or, at least, programs are likely to have to rely on the disproportionate use of adjunct faculty. At the same time, relying on any group (such as adult learners) to achieve an increase in income may be perceived as a necessary evil, so it is easy to understand how situations regarding adult programs are often likely to create additional tension on the campus among faculty and administrators.

Lack of Institutional Support

But the most significant problems with adult programs appear when there is little or no foundational support from the institution. That is, when a school determines that it will rely on adult learners to supplement income but then doesn't provide the philosophical, historical, and andragogical (the adult learner version of "pedagogical"—see Chapter 2) foundations for its faculty and support staff, problems will almost certainly follow (and continue, unless these issues are addressed). Indeed, successful adult programs, like any other successful entity on the college campus, are inevitably based upon best practices and longitudinal research, especially as established over the past 25 years. However, faculty and administrative perceptions do not always take these efforts into consideration. Often this can be directly attributed to how the program is perceived in the first place—and frequently, adult programs are merely seen as the institution's cash cow.

The Cash Cow Syndrome

The unvarnished fact of the matter is that, unfortunately, the academy has too often treated adult learners primarily as a lucrative source of income. Because these programs typically require less overhead and diminished services, there are abundant examples of colleges and universities that opt for adult programs merely to satisfy financial rather than philosophical needs. The frequent, disproportionate use of adjunct faculty, bundled with other reduced maintenance costs associated with the sort of shortened (i.e., accelerated) classroom time commonly utilized by adult learner programs account for much of the academic cost effectiveness of these programs. Adult students, with their dual part-time and commuter status, tend to require little from the institution in terms of those facilities (e.g., dormitories or recreational space), infrastructure, or services normally associated with 18- to 22-year-old students. As a result, adult programs are likely to be treated as the campus cash cow by those institutions that are merely seeking short-term revenue gains.

A common experience when a new adult program is proposed on the campus is for the members of the board to be well versed when it comes to the income side of the matter, but when asked about necessary support systems, sensitivity to the special needs of adult learners, or other initiatives to consider for this population, they suddenly become less articulate. Even worse are those faculty members who have already spent the money that such programs are likely to generate, but don't want to accept courses offered to adults as equivalent should one of the adult students suddenly decide to follow a day or traditional program track instead. In fact, a lack of faculty investment can be very damaging to any program.

Lack of Faculty Investment

Unfortunately, adult programs frequently encounter a lack of philosophical investment and respect on the part of full-time faculty. In the more extreme examples (see the case study at the end of this chapter), faculty members may even co-opt their responsibilities and disassociate themselves entirely from the adult learner program. But at times faculty members and administrators do respond with more subtlety to adult learning initiatives. In some instances, one can observe a faculty dichotomy in response to the adult program where one portion of the full-time faculty may be fully committed to supporting the special needs of the adult learners while the remainder of the community may be passive or do very little to demonstrate their support at all. Indeed, this situation may pose a special problem since no consensual response is more likely to stunt momentum and eventually erode the effectiveness of the adult program. At the very least, this situation engenders the specter of marginality and the lack of power and privilege frequently encountered in adult education as noted by Sheared (1994).

Philosophical Differences: Traditional Versus Adult Students

There are numerous schools where the dichotomy between advocates for adult learners and those who support the notion that the academy exists primarily for 18- to 22-year-old students has created a notable level of tension. The 21st century is already characterized by dramatic changes on the campus with the attendant challenge to the status quo that, in itself, may even be increasing tension at many schools. There are a number of contributing factors that may account for the apparent escalation of friction of support between adult and traditional learners: 1) a rather dramatic shift in demographics, 2) a new pattern of expectations and thinking in the workplace, 3) new delivery systems that make learning more accessible than ever before, and 4) new proven formats (such as accelerated learning, distance learning, corporate partnerships, and prior learning assessment) that often tend to challenge past practices. Of course, these issues all represent change on the campus—something that the academy has seldom ever embraced with enthusiasm under any circumstances (Abeles, 2001; Greenberg, 2001). While all of these issues will be examined throughout this book, they also serve as a reminder that the 21st century poses powerful changes to an academy that has "remained remarkably consistent for more than 200 years" (Taylor, 2001, p. B14). As a result, stakeholders are encouraged to rethink all aspects of the entire educational process, especially including such topics as 1) teaching versus learning, 2) governance and infrastructure, 3) partnerships (in and out of the academy), 4) research, and 5) curriculum.

The following case study, the first of several used to illustrate important elements covered in the text, represents an amalgam of unfortunate endeavors some schools have undertaken in pursuit of the lucrative adult market. In almost all cases, those schools that are already facing fiscal challenges or experiencing some form of financial risk are more likely to see some aspects of adult programs as an easy solution to their problem. Although this case serves to remind us that adult programs need to be guided by best practice principles and benchmark models, there are, unfortunately, too many instances of cases similar to Leeward University.

Case Study: Leeward University

Leeward University is located in the suburbs about 35 miles from a large city. When the school opened in 1950, its location emphasized its mission—to provide a sound education for high school graduates within its immediate area. At the time, the population in the area was sufficient to support the modest school, creating a good fit for all involved. The school gradually grew until the year before its 40th anniversary when the trustees approved a plan that set 2,000 students as an enrollment target. It was about this time that the region began to experience significant growth due to the influx of many new corporate headquarters. (Today, there are over 100 corporate headquarters or research and development centers within a 20-mile radius of the school.) Even though this rapid expansion initially benefited the university with a significant spurt in enrollment, two unforeseen consequences eventually changed the institution dramatically.

Due to the significant increase in jobs, many more families moved into the immediate area. This, in turn, created a situation where Leeward accepted more students than the infrastructure was designed to sustain, thereby bringing about very rapid growth of both faculty and facilities. At the same time, some of the major universities located in the nearby city began opening satellite campuses near Leeward to compete for their students. These schools also recognized that many of the corporations were encouraging their workers to seek degrees and/or certificates, so they brought their established adult programs designed to meet during the evenings and weekend as well.

Three years ago, Leeward University found itself in a serious financial bind. First, they had felt compelled to expand too rapidly to meet demand due to the increased regional population. Then, the competing schools drew away so many of their students that the Leeward resources and infrastructures were underutilized, which put them in financial jeopardy. At this point, the administration, in an effort to stabilize the institution and infuse the school with money, decided to offer evening and weekend courses.

The president of Leeward, Dr. Bertram Marlowe, decided to seek out a firm that specialized in outsourcing adult learning packages, since the school had no previous experience with the adult market. By providing all of the details, from marketing support to curriculum, from admission guidelines to new degree programs designed to meet the specific needs of the regional adult population, and from prepackaged schedules to recommended criteria for prior learning assessment, the company offered a package that seemed to entail little risk to the institution with a guarantee of approximately 40% of the income. There was, however, a sense of urgency that Dr. Marlowe shared with his faculty: "Leeward is facing a serious financial crisis. This company is offering us a solution that, based on their projections, will generate significant revenue in a short time, and thus, allow us to continue with our primary mission. To do so, however, I need your approval."

When faculty learned that they would not be required to actively participate in teaching any of the courses, they were relieved. The schedule utilized a five-week cohort model, meeting one night per week with a study group. Even though many faculty members expressed reservations about the validity of trying to cover a semester's material in five weeks, all but two of them took a wait-and-see attitude. In the meantime, with promises of increased revenue to meet their operating budgets and expectations of actual raises for the first time in three years, the faculty voted in favor of the new program.

With the company's assistance, the program was offered to the first group of adult students a brief five months later. By including the two full-time faculty along with nine adjunct faculty, the courses were in place for the first year, and 11 students formed the first cohort. Although this number was significantly less than the target of 20 to 25 that the company had based its financial model upon, everyone was reassured that the enrollment would increase over the next two years as more cohorts were added.

By the end of the second year, in preparation for a regional accrediting team's visit to evaluate the viability of the program, the following facts became suddenly clear.

- Only six students in the original cohort actually completed their studies to graduate (rendering the "income" a small operating loss instead).
- The next four cohorts that had been scheduled to begin every five months had not experienced the anticipated growth the company had envisioned. Instead, the average cohort contained only ten students.

- The reduction of class contact and extensive use of adjunct faculty had severely challenged the credibility of the program. After teaching one term, both full-time faculty members decided to no longer participate, though they were quite vocal among their colleagues about the problems they had encountered. At this point, the full-time faculty didn't want to be associated with the adult program, though they were still hoping it would make a profit.
- The use of prior learning assessment had quickly become an admission's ploy to attract more adults by giving them wholesale credit (approximately 30 hours), basically for having lived their life.
- Independent from the accrediting team, the federal government was reviewing some of the policies employed by the outsource company regarding student aid.
- Recently, the faculty voiced their profound concern regarding the adult curriculum and level of instruction that was being utilized for the adult program. This issue finally came into focus when one of the students in the cohort decided to complete her studies as a day student. The faculty decided that they were unwilling to accept the courses she had already completed in the evening as part of her transcript.

After the student came to him with her complaint, President Marlowe intervened. Upon further investigation, the program was discontinued abruptly before the fifth cohort ever had the chance to begin. Currently, Leeward University is operating under a stringency budget.

Conclusion

There is substantial evidence that more colleges and universities will face fiscal problems during the next 20 years than ever before. Many colleges are simply not expected to survive the challenges of a new century that is likely to mark the most dramatic changes higher education has ever faced. Because many of these challenges will relate to money, the cash cow syndrome will certainly become an inevitable solution for some of these schools. Although many administrators may perceive adult programs as a quick fix to their problems, adult programs that lack substantial foundations and support will only serve to further jeopardize the institution.

●●●●●

Placing Adult Learners in a 21st Century Perspective

Many discussions have focused on how the academy might benefit from the experiences leaders in adult education have faced and solved, since the academy now confronts many of the same issues, only with a greater level of magnitude.

Institutional Models

Although it may not be immediately apparent, there is substantial evidence that the adult learning movement is, in many ways, at the vanguard leading higher education into the 21st century. Benchmark adult programs have long been recognized for their ability to provide flexible, responsive, entrepreneurial models. At the same time, higher education is undergoing the most profound changes in its entire history. According to Frank Newman (1999), director of the Futures Project at Brown University:

> Higher education in this country is in a period of change and turbulence that is likely to bring about substantial transformation of the system of higher education and, for many students, the nature of "going to college."
>
> A number of converging forces are serving as a catalyst for change. These include: changing demographics, including a growing demand for more advanced skills for essentially all of the workforce; rapid growth of technology; and the advent of new providers of higher education services (both for-profit and nonprofit, new institutions as well as established institutions taking on new roles). The traditional institutions of higher education—the nonprofit public and private colleges and universities—are vulnerable to these forces of change because, in some critical dimensions, they are out of sync with societal needs. (p. 1)

What is perhaps most compelling about this quote is that the benchmark adult learning programs have been responding to these kinds of converging forces for almost 20 years. The very real challenge, however, is whether members of the academy will recognize how well suited model adult programs have been to respond to these converging forces in the past. But as previously noted, many colleges and universities have been unwilling to recognize the significance of adult programs thus far, so there is a strong likelihood that these same schools will be unwilling to turn to these programs as resources to assist them in these new challenges. But clearly, adult learning programs are in the right place at the right time as exemplified by a remarkable corollary with another 20th century educational movement that has experienced a notable transformation within a short period: jazz education. Because adult learning shares much in common with jazz education, both in terms of its apparent influence and impact within and upon the learning community, a closer examination of the profound transformation that has taken place in jazz education may prove useful to illustrate the evolution adult learning is currently undergoing as well.

Before exploring the remarkable similarities between adult learning programs and jazz education, it is important to emphasize that the reader is not required to have any special background or knowledge about jazz in order to see how the success of one program (jazz education) might serve as the model for the other. In fact, this comparison is really a systems analysis rather than reference to a musical style. If anything, the significance of jazz education made an initial impact slightly earlier than the adult learning movement in terms of when it began to gather momentum and achieve a level of credibility and recognition at most institutions of higher education.

How Jazz Education Serves as a Prototype for Adult Learning in the 21st Century

Jazz has been described as America's classic art form; however, this description does not reflect the intensity of resistance the music and musicians encountered during its formative stages. Because it relied on improvisation and utilized musicians from diverse backgrounds, members of the status quo (i.e., classical musicians) often openly treated it with disdain and contempt. Indeed, by using terms like "classical" or "traditional" to describe nonjazz music, the term "jazz" came to be used by many people in a pejorative manner. Consequently, for most of the 20th century, jazz music and musicians could be described as marginalized among their fellow musicians and critics. This is only the first of many similarities between jazz and adult education.

> Note how faculty and administrators seeking to maintain the status quo on their campus are likely to employ the same strategy when it comes to their reference to "traditional" students on the one hand as opposed to "nontraditional," "commuter," "transfer," and other terms that emphasize the "otherness" of the adult learner. Although such labels may seem innocent and descriptive, they are, in fact, political and powerful in how they convey lack of status, affect expectations, and influence the actions of educators, especially in what they value or diminish about learners. (Sissel, Hansman, & Kasworm, 2001, pp. 19–20)

Although jazz was introduced to the general public in the early portion of the 20th century, it wasn't until the 1930s when it began to gain widespread attention. That is not to say, however, that it achieved widespread acceptance—especially in the established music world. In fact, it was in the 1960s when music education was suffering a significant decline in enrollment and participation that the concept of jazz in the schools began to be introduced more systematically as a response to the enrollment problem. Previously, attempts at jazz education were limited almost exclusively to a hardy, dedicated, and determined group of practitioners who often met stiff opposition.

Even though the 1970s testify to the steady growth of enrollment among music students who found performing and learning about jazz relevant, there were many strong pockets of resistance among educators. At the same time that music students of all ages began resonating and responding to the sorts of skills and challenges the music presented, music educators, who represented the establishment, frequently offered significant obstacles and objections to jazz education. As late as the early 1980s, some famous conservatories had signs posted on their practice room doors indicating that "jazz music will result in the student being expelled" from their program.

By the late 1980s, the National Association of Jazz Educators, formed in the US in 1969, changed its name to the International Association of Jazz Educators. This action was taken as a reflection of both the success of the movement and also its worldwide pervasiveness. Today, jazz education is incredibly dynamic in all parts of the world. Ultimately, the success of this educational phenomenon is probably less about the music itself and more about how the students' experiences help prepare them to be successful in nearly all aspects of a dramatically changed world today.

An Information Age Perspective

It may be helpful to use the perspective of Alvin Toffler's (1980) book, *The Third Wave,* to help understand how jazz education "suddenly" became so important to the educational system. Try to think of jazz education as a phenomenon—the byproduct of the sea change associated with moving from a second wave (industrial revolution) orientation to that of the information age (third wave) perspective where much greater reliance is placed on the individual. Whereas previous music instruction and performance had relied on accurate and precise *replication* above all else, the essence of jazz is *improvisation,* where the individual is expected to solve problems independently and organically so that the solutions are neither predictable nor intended to be repeated from one performance to the next. In other words, a whole new level of creativity—with emphasis on the individual learner—emerged in jazz instruction but served as a prototype for learning, growing, and succeeding in all aspects of life. Interestingly enough, these are the very skills that 21st century leaders, workers, and students are being asked to display. At the same time, the model adult learner-centered programs that rely heavily on flexibility, responsiveness to learners' needs, and entrepreneurial approaches are being asked to develop the very same skills. Consequently, adult programs may wish to draw from those lessons learned by jazz educators.

The Adult Learner Corollary

Because adult learners seek direct, practical responses to their needs, because they can be more demanding than 18- to 22-year-olds since they are more likely to see themselves as consumers or customers, and because adult learners' needs tend to be more fluid than their younger counterparts, adult learner programs face special problems that position them especially well in the 21st century. The model benchmark adult programs have had to learn how to become quickly responsive (especially to customer complaints), flexible, open and sensitive listeners, and adept at developing new products (e.g., certificates, courses, presentations, degrees) according to an ever-shifting set of demands. These are the sorts of activities good college-level adult education programs have been doing on a regular basis almost since their inception. That is, the programs have been involved with entrepreneurial endeavors. Now, the academy is being asked to adapt some version of this model institution-wide, and many people believe that adult programs will provide the prototypical model. Here's where the academy of the future might be particularly wise to rely on the good work adult programs have already been fully immersed in as entrepreneurs. There can be little doubt that the academy is in the midst of a remarkable transformation that is likely to create even more profound changes than any of those our culture has endured just since the beginning of the new century.

Clifford Baden (2002) affirms the entrepreneurial role of continuing education while indicating the growing likelihood of colleges and universities willing to enter into what he describes as "the new wave of entrepreneurship [that] may test the limits of what society views as the proper role or purpose of colleges and universities" (p. 46). And once again, he confirms the level of influence for this phenomenon that can be attributed to continuing education when he states:

> Continuing education is the unit on campus that has traditionally had its finger on the pulse of the marketplace and has learned how to bridge the gap between the university and the rest of the community, especially the for-profit sector. (p. 45)

The Academy of the Future: The Growing Need for Entrepreneurialism

Numerous sources are now calling for the academy to utilize a more entrepreneurial approach in order to be both competitive and responsive to a new student profile in the 21st century. Steven D. Crow, executive director of the Higher Learning Commission of the North Central Association of Colleges and Schools, in his 2001 keynote address to the commission's consultant/evaluator corps, articulated the following vision.

> Our colleges and universities are so unaccustomed to entrepreneurialism, responsiveness, and creative collaboration that they do not always do a very good job at any of them. Many of us still cringe when we witness it because it seems, well, tawdry and suspect. (p. 8)

Near the end of his observations, he provided one further insight:

> As I look to 2010, I see that technology is changing almost every single workplace, requiring that people not only have higher-level competencies in order to succeed in the working environment but also are capable of engaging in the self-directed lifelong learning necessary for flexible responsiveness to change. In short, the new workplace makes demands for different kinds of competencies and higher learning experiences. We must listen carefully to those who try to define the learning they need and then we must create those learning opportunities quickly and, often, with the help of others. (p. 9)

The strategies necessary to respond to that call are precisely what benchmark adult learning programs have already been actively engaging and applying in their everyday activities for up to three decades. Although colleges and universities may be somewhat slow to seize the best practices of adult learner programs as their institutional model, there can be little doubt of the appropriateness of that model and the potential for institutional success when one objectively examines what Crow calls "the flexible responsiveness to change" as the criterion. Indeed, flexibility, responsiveness—not only to change but also to all the needs of the adult learners (in other words, an entrepreneurial perspective)—and learner-centered programs have long been the hallmarks of adult learning. But the entrepreneurial spirit and attitude that have served to support and sustain adult learning models are really comprised of a number of contributing factors. Although not all of the items listed below may fit into any single program, all successful adult learner focused programs have included at least some of the following:

- Risk-taking
- Creativity and innovation
- Strategic thinking and planning
- Vision
- A win/win approach
- Partnerships and collaborations

- Thinking beyond real or perceived barriers—especially when it comes to funding and support
- Flexibility
- Responsiveness

Guiding Principles

In its report to the Board of Trustees of the Higher Learning Commission, the Task Force on Adult Degree Completion Programs and the Award of Credit for Prior Learning at the Baccalaureate Level (2000) noted: "Adult degree completion programs have become increasingly relevant within the higher education community and they are growing at a rapid pace across the nation" (p. 1). Although the remainder of their report primarily focuses on the role and exemplary practices of adult learning programs within the context of the institution, a few observations at the conclusion expand to a more comprehensive perspective directed toward institutions.

> Lifelong learning is not a catch phrase or a fad but rather a trend that marks a significant change in the behavior of increasing numbers of adults who have come to value the need for continuous learning
>
> Much is happening in the adult education movement today, and institutions can ill afford to operate adult degree completion programs on the periphery of their traditional curricula. Each institution must decide the scope of the business it is in, and plan and operate accordingly. (p. 10)

While the task force is to be commended for its efforts, practitioners in adult learning programs are likely to respond that these observations have long been encompassed in the best practices and guiding principles of model adult learning programs (See Chapter 4). Indeed, taking a lead from the comments previously attributed to Steve Crow, individuals who work with adult learners are likely to conclude that his comments about institutions have already resonated with adult learning programs for some time. To return again to Crow (2001), he also emphasizes the importance of building learner-centered communities and thinking about the institution more as an entrepreneur:

> But there is a new culture emerging within higher education. It is one in which the learning of students is central; it is one in which hierarchical structures give way to collaborative teamwork; it is one in which institutional boundaries blur when cooperation and collaboration provide better service to students; it is one in which success is measured by the achievement of clearly defined goals; and it is one that continues to hold as fundamental a commitment to unfettered intellectual inquiry and academic freedom. (p. 8)

These same individuals sensitive to adult learning will quickly recognize that this description is consistent with established best practices and benchmarks that have defined adult programs during the past few years (again, see Chapter 4 for more detailed examples of guidelines and principles for model adult programs).

Lessons Learned

Although managing institutional change in higher education may be one of the greater challenges of the 21st century, adult learning programs have been relying upon organic or kaleidoscopic change to define many of their initiatives for more than 20 years. In fact, their survival has often relied upon their creativity, their flexibility, and their capacity to listen carefully before responding with what their constituents are seeking. In other words, they have evolved through entrepreneurial strategies, initiatives, and thinking. To cite a few examples:

- Many adult programs serve as the primary residence or center for various forms of distance learning initiatives.
- Lifelong learning has begun to take on greater significance as adult programs seek to expand their constituencies in all directions.
- The delivery of courses has often expanded to anywhere, anytime in an effort to respond to new lifestyles.
- The format of these courses has likewise extended to a full gamut of options, from highly compressed and intense, to extending beyond the conventional semester.
- Perhaps the most extreme example of such initiatives resides within those courses that are asynchronous.

- Many programs are based upon partnerships and collaborations that might have seemed far-fetched until recently.

Reinventing the Wheel

"Those who do not remember the past are condemned to repeat it." Those prophetic words by George Santanyana have been ringing in my ears as I began collecting various resources in preparation for writing this book. Hidden among this collection was a 50-page book published in 1973 titled *The Learning Society: A Report of the Study on Continuing Education and the Future.* Initially I ignored it, but after completing the first draft of this book, I examined the text one final time.

The Learning Society was published after the formation of four task forces met in 1972 at the Center for Continuing Education at the University of Notre Dame to address the following topics: continuing education and social responsibility, continuing education and public affairs, continuing education and the university, and continuing education for new knowledge and the professions. The 24 individuals involved with these task forces represent a prestigious array of college and university presidents and leaders from that decade, along with some representation from various components of the government and corporate world as well. The task forces "examined developments in their respective areas of concern and recommended courses of action to improve the quality and accessibility of continuing education, measured against the national need" (*The Learning Society,* 1973, p. ix).

Much of higher education and adult learning has changed in the 30 years since this book's publication, but most of the recommendations read as if they were written today. As such, they provide a fascinating insight into how far adult learning has come and how much more still needs to be done. One other interesting aspect of this document: While the titles of the center and task forces refer to continuing education, most of the references under the recommendations are more likely to relate to lifelong learning. This suggests a breakthrough in thinking about the topic that may have taken place during the discussions. The following is a summary of the recommendations.

Curricular changes: These should be designed to help assure that each student develops the ability to participate in lifelong learning.

1) A substantial part of the undergraduate curriculum in every subject matter area should be redesigned to help students learn how to carry out a program of self-education and lifelong learning.

2) The responsibilities among institutions for inculcating skills and attitudes favoring learning differ according to institutional type and purpose; these different responsibilities should be recognized and appropriate steps taken to meet them.

Public policies: Policies that underwrite, promote and essentially guarantee the widest possible access to learning opportunity should be implemented.

3) The Congress should enact a universal bill of educational rights that would guarantee to every citizen access to the widest possible educational opportunities.

4) Changes are needed in public policies to promote lifelong learning through released time from employment, tax deductions or tax credits, and retraining programs that promise new careers. Public policy should encourage the use of school and college facilities for community education purposes.

5) Model programs of in-service education should be developed for public employees and elected officials.

Institutional responses: Institutions should strive to take actions that promote universal access to continuous learning and greater efficiency and social impact in the use of resources.

6) Consortia of institutions should be established on a local, regional, and national basis to pool resources for continuing education with the aim of making sure that virtually all citizens have access to continuous learning of high quality.

7) Each college or university should continuously renew its commitments as well as identify the resources necessary to meet its responsibility in lifelong learning. Account should be taken of the changing educational needs of groups to be served, and strong efforts should be made to improve access programs.

8) Colleges and universities should contribute to finding solutions for the pressing social and environmental problems of our time, together with increasing the educational services available for disadvantaged groups.

9) Efforts should be made to promote and improve continuing education for professional people through the use of special incentives. Retraining programs should be developed in areas of surplus manpower.

10) Institutions should encourage the development of materials and educational programs in citizenship and consumer affairs for the use of a wide public.

11) The centers for continuing education associated with colleges and universities should assert new leadership in bringing resources to bear on new concepts and needs in lifelong learning.

12) There should be established a commission or center that would promote the aims of the Learning Society, based on the recommendations of this report. (*The Learning Society,* 1973, pp. 43–45)

Examining the contents of this book—especially the recommendations—is like opening a time capsule. At least ten of the visionary participants were, at some point in their career, presidents of some of the nation's largest universities. One might assume that this group of nationally prominent figures exerted their influence to help change lifelong learning programs in meaningful ways. But sometimes, truly significant changes require being in the right place at the right time. The 21st century may be the ideal time to see many of these recommendations become realities in dynamic and meaningful ways.

Conclusion

As the academy seeks solutions to the dramatic changes it will inevitably be called upon to make in the new century, it may or may not seek adult learning programs to serve as models. Whether the academy embraces the adult model or even pursues the entrepreneurial perspective they typically exemplify, there is no doubt that adult programs represent one of the more dynamic change agents in higher education today. There are many examples of how these programs have already provided solid alternatives to the status quo and therefore, the lessons learned from these programs deserve our further consideration. Adult programs have now provided many meaningful baselines and models that should serve as instructive examples for any educator seeking to prepare his or her school with strategies for success in the 21st century.

Furthermore, one additional factor has become an important consideration regarding today's lifelong learner: Students of all ages are now expected to recycle their learning throughout their entire career. That is, an incoming 18-year-old student today is expected to continue college-level learning forever—thus making lifelong learning truly meaningful for both students and the institution.

I also need to add one final word about the correlation between adult learning programs and jazz education that became particularly clear during the preparation of this book. Having served as book review editor for *Jazz Educators Journal* for more than 15 years, I was able to observe first hand the gradual increase in the number of related books being published during that period. By the time I completed my duties in 2001, I was reviewing approximately 50 jazz education–related books each year. When I began, I was fortunate if I was able to find one-third that amount written at a sufficient level to warrant reviewing.

Likewise, there has been a noticeable increase in publications relating to adult learners and lifelong learning programs in recent years. Just as with jazz education, there are a few nuggets that were published more than ten years ago that have helped define adult learners and the programs that support them. These books tend to be written by the trailblazers in the field, carefully composed when the discipline was still at the formative stage. But more recently, research and authors have reflected the greater complexity that comprises adult learner programs in the 21st century. In some ways, making sense of that complexity poses a greater challenge than ever before. But the effort is likely to pay off in significant dividends since having a better grasp of higher education and the role adult programs are likely to contribute to the academy of the future is what is at stake. And at no time in the history of the academy has the enrollment and nurturing of adult learners been more critical than at this time.

References

Abeles, T. P. (2001). Partnering and cultural change. *On the Horizon, 9* (4), 2–3.

Baden, C. (2002, Winter). The new entrepreneurship: What impact? *The Journal of Continuing Higher Education, 50* (1), 45–47.

Canja, E. T. (2002, Spring). Lifelong learning: Challenges & opportunities. *CAEL Forum and News,* 26–29.

Crow, S. D. (2001, March). *Serving the common good: Consultant-evaluators in the heart of peer review.* Retrieved June 5, 2001, from http://www.ncahigherlearningcommission.org/AnnualMeeting/archive/

Greenberg, D. (2001, July/August). The Trojan Horse of education. *On the Horizon, 9,* 4, 1, 4–5.

The learning society: A report of the study on continuing education and the future. (1973). Notre Dame, IN: Center for Continuing Education, University of Notre Dame.

Lovett, C. M. (2002, March/April). Cracks in the bedrock: Can U.S. higher education remain number one? *Change,* 11–15.

Newman, F. (1999, March 5). *The transformation of American higher education.* Retrieved August 22, 2001, from http://www.futuresproject.org/publications/american_education.pdf

Sheared, V. (1994). Giving voice: A womanist construction. In E. Hayes & S. A. J. Colin III (Eds.), *Confronting racism and sexism in adult continuing education.* San Francisco, CA: Jossey-Bass.

Sissel, P. A., Hansman, C. A., & Kasworm, C. E. (2001, Fall). The politics of neglect: Adult learners in higher education. *New Directions for Adult and Continuing Education, 91,* 17–27.

Task Force on Adult Degree Completion Programs. (2000, June). *Adult degree completion programs.* Retrieved June 5, 2001, from http://www.ncacihe.org/resources/adctf/ADCPRept.pdf

Taylor, M. C. (2001, December 14). Unplanned obsolescence and the new network culture. *The Chronicle of Higher Education,* pp. B14–B16.

Toffler, A. (1980). *The third wave.* New York, NY: Random House.

2

Adult Learners: Who They Are and How They Differ From the Traditional Student

Overview

Adult learners (typically described as 25 or older) now comprise more than 45% of the total enrollment in colleges and universities (even more if you include corporate universities and other learning/training situations). In order to provide a suitable adult program, it is especially important for faculty and administrators to understand this population—their needs and characteristics along with the special challenges they pose since they are a unique population. Unfortunately, too many campus leaders have either ignored adult learners or treated them like second-class citizens. No institution can afford this behavior in today's highly competitive market. Indeed, many of the more successful colleges and universities today are consciously examining how to more fully integrate adult learners into their mission and community.

When they seek admission to the college or university, adult learners draw upon their years of experience—either as savvy customers or simply as seasoned individuals, making them distinctly different from their younger classmates. In fact, almost every aspect of their characteristics and expectations stands in stark contrast to the traditional (i.e., 18- to 22-year-old) student.

Not only are they formidable when it comes to the sorts of expectations they bring to the campus, their entire approach to learning is different as well. Perhaps the single largest misconception regarding adult learners may be that a "cookie cutter" approach to their learning is somehow acceptable. Again, it is critical to enter the classroom with an adult-sensitive attitude and approach. This chapter helps explain why that strategy is a good idea and what makes adult learners both different and important in the 21st century academy.

Definition and Characteristics of Adult Learners

Not by Age Alone

There is probably no more compelling evidence of the transformation taking place on the campus than the rather sobering demographic profile of today's student. Despite the fact that the majority of faculty members and administrators may wish to think and talk about the "typical" student being 18 to 22 years old, demographic projections suggest that by the year 2005 more than 50% of all students will be 25 or older—the technical definition for adult learners according to the Commission for a Nation of Lifelong Learners (1997).

Historically, adult learners have long been classified primarily by their age, as though that distinction alone defined them. But as long ago as the early 20th century, Alfred North Whitehead (1929), the noted English philosopher who championed the cause of adult learners (and for whom Whitehead College, an adult learner program at the University of Redlands, was named), suggested the importance of utility in education, supplemented by experiential learning in order to support relevance and application within a student's life. In fact, he is generally recognized as one of the first educators to comprehend that different individuals develop at different levels and according to a diverse set of circumstances. (Today, we are probably more likely to attribute this phenomenon to those individuals who we perceive as being "late bloomers.")

Notable distinctions mark the differences between an adult learner and the conventional 18- to 22-year-old student. Indeed, any instructor who has had the opportunity to have both student groups in his or her classroom will quickly confirm that each group tends to behave differently as well as to express different expectations from the instructor and the course. Furthermore—due to a number of circumstances described below—adult learners are likely to demonstrate behavior that reflects greater levels of urgency and higher motivation than their younger fellow students.

The typical adult is most likely to attend school as a part-time student and work full-time in the sort of position where, as a result of completing studies, he or she hopes to achieve a promotion and/or an increase in salary. Therefore, adult learners are likely to express their sense of urgency at a more visceral or emotional level than their younger counterparts. Another reason for their stronger sense of purpose is the feeling that they experience a sense of reduced opportunities and options at a certain point in their lives. On the other hand, some authorities suggest that these students are simply demonstrating the same techniques in the classroom that are designed to assist adults in coping with the accelerated pace of change we are all encountering in our daily lives. But whatever the explanation, adult students almost always express their sense of urgency and impatience, either overtly or with some subtlety. (A future chapter will further explore some of the underlying aspects of this phenomenon.)

Malcolm Knowles: The Pioneer of Adult Education

Malcolm Knowles pioneered the field of adult learning in the United States during the second half of the 20th century, devoting almost his entire life to adult education. His extensive efforts as a writer and speaker directly influenced a multitude of practitioners, while many of his works continue, even today, to define the nature and phenomenon of the adult learner (Carlson, 1989). Knowles based many of his later books on the concept of "andragogy"—a term that he appropriated from its use in Europe. Although the European definition and interpretation of andragogy focused on "adult accompanying adult in the learning process" (Carlson, 1989, p. 5), Knowles redefined the word to mean, "an emerging technology for adult learning" (Carlson, 1989, p. 5). Eventually he developed a seven-step process that encompassed andragogy and required educators to:

- Set a cooperative learning climate.
- Create mechanisms for mutual planning.
- Arrange for a diagnosis of learner needs and interests.
- Enable the formulation of learning objectives based on the diagnosed needs and interests.
- Design sequential activities for achieving the objectives.
- Execute the design by selecting methods, materials, and resources.
- Evaluate the quality of the learning experience while rediagnosing needs for further learning. (Carlson, 1989, pp. 5–6)

Although Knowles's original works contrast the characteristics of adults and those of 18- to 22-year-olds, the focus here is exclusively on the adult learner in order to better emphasize what makes the adult learner distinctive (Knowles, 1984). The original contrast between adult learners and 18- to 22-year-olds is provided in Appendix 2.1.

Characteristics of Adult Learners

Adult learners are *autonomous* and *self-directed.* They need to be free to have a sense of control over their own learning. Their teachers should actively involve adults in the learning process and serve as facilitators for them. Specifically, instructors are encouraged to get participants' perspectives about what topics to cover and let them work on projects that reflect their interests. Typically, adults are eager to assume responsibility for presentations and group leadership. Instructors are most likely to be effective when they enable their students, guiding them from a starting point that draws on their own knowledge rather than simply supplying them with facts.

Adult learners have accumulated a foundation of *life experiences* and knowledge that may include work-related activities, interest-based experiences, family responsibilities, and previous education. They need to connect learning to their knowledge/experience base. To help them do so, instructors may wish to draw out adult learners' experience and knowledge relevant to the topic. Faculty are encouraged to relate theories and concepts to the students and recognize the value of experience in learning.

Adult learners are *goal-oriented.* Upon enrolling in a course or a program, they usually know what goals they want to attain. Therefore, they appreciate an educational program that is organized and has clearly defined elements. Instructors who show adult learners how the class will help them attain their goals early in the course often describe such a strategy as one of the most productive. At the same time, because adult learners tend to have little margin for error in their busy schedules, they are less adaptable to change in the midst of their efforts. Instructors who add new assignments or change requirements—requests that are probably not unreasonable in more conventional classrooms—are likely to create significant problems in a classroom with adult learners since they will have devoted a much greater portion of their energy in planning ahead. This is also a strong justification for creating a very clear, precise, and accurate syllabus with every expectation specifically spelled out well in advance.

Adult learners are *relevancy-oriented.* They tend to feel that they must see a reason for learning something or understand the connection between the learning event and some aspect of their life. From their perspective, learning has to be applicable to their work or other responsibilities to be of value to them. Adult learners may be reluctant to extend time and energy (two precious commodities for them) on any assignment that doesn't offer them residual benefits. Therefore, successful instructors often identify objectives for adult learners even before the course begins—again, in the best instances, as a part of their syllabus. The purpose is to demonstrate a relationship between coursework and "real life" for the students. Often, relevancy can be addressed in the classroom by the instructor who enables learners to create projects that reflect their own interests.

Adult learners are *practical,* focusing on the aspects of a lesson most useful to them in their work or personal life. They may not be interested in knowledge for its own sake. This is particularly true among those students who are only beginning their studies. However, many adult learners eventually do evolve into lifelong learners, where the issue of practicality may diminish due to their wanting to learn for the pure pleasure of learning.

Though applicable to all learners, adult learners particularly express the need to be shown *respect.* Wise instructors acknowledge the wealth of experiences that adult learners bring to the classroom, even if their knowledge base is deficient. These adults expect to be treated as equals based on their experience and general understanding. Furthermore, they assume they will be allowed to voice their opinions freely in class and those opinions will be regarded as having some value. In many instances, adult learners are also much more *assertive* than their younger classmates. Since perceptions are subjective, when adult learners perceive they are not being treated with respect they may be more likely to act on those perceptions. Treating all students equally, with sensitivity and objectivity, are strategies many faculty members employ in order to address the issues of respect and assertiveness.

Obviously, any combination of these traits can be a challenge for faculty members. They may be intimidating or problematic for some faculty members whose interactions with younger students may have demanded less effort than that required by adult learners. When these characteristics are coupled with the willingness of many adult learners to be more outspoken and assertive in the classroom then their younger classmates, they offer a profile that some faculty members may find less desirable. Consequently, there may be some instructors who are well suited to work with adult learners since "fit" can be a significant issue, while others may be reluctant to make the kinds of adjustments these students are likely to require. Future chapters will reveal how to maximize this relationship for those professors seeking to improve their effectiveness.

As indicated by Ross-Gordon (2002), ". . . choices about teaching adults are and should be made based on numerous considerations, including factors related to content, learner background knowledge, and learner personal characteristics" (p. 85) in order to become effective teachers. To accomplish this objective, instructors must be intentional in both their reflective practice and investment in transformative teaching practices. This, in turn, helps create a learner-centered environment with greater sensitivity and appreciation for the adult learner.

The Importance of "Mattering"

One further adult learner characteristic, *mattering,* has been identified by Schlossberg, Lynch, and Chickering (1989) as especially important for adult learners when it comes to their ability to persevere or succeed at their task. There are five dimensions of mattering, each provided below with a description. Criteria for each is supplied to assist faculty members or administrators in the assessment of their own programs.

Attention: Takes place when we feel that we command interest or the notice of another person.

- Students have a place on campus to get mail or messages, and store their belongings.
- Students receive thoughtful messages on papers.
- Students are encouraged to know one another by name.

Importance: Takes place when we are the object of a person's (or program's) concern and when we believe that a person cares about what we want, think, and do.

- School recognizes the importance of student advising and makes appropriate provisions regarding accessibility.
- School provides good information and support for financial aid for adult learners.

- Student absences are noted and faculty members are encouraged to take appropriate action to signal their concern or express how such absences might interfere with their success.

Dependence: Takes place when we feel that others depend upon us.

- Students are expected and encouraged to participate in class discussions and interactions.
- Students check on one another when absences occur.

Ego-extension: Takes place when we feel that others will be proud of our accomplishments and disappointed with our failures.

- Professors indicate their interest in students even after they have completed their course or left school.

Appreciation: Takes place when we feel that others are thankful for who we are and what we do.

- Students are able to receive credit for what they've learned from life experiences through prior learning assessment, the College-Level Examination Program (CLEP), and other means.
- The administration treats the adult learner with the same support and understanding as they extend to traditional-aged students.

In many ways, Jim typifies the adult learner. As a traditional student, he merely saw the pursuit of his college education as a means to an end, since his primary focus was on baseball. Because he wasn't severely inconvenienced when he left college, he only thought about what a college degree might have offered him as an abstraction. Therefore, he seldom even thought about returning to school until he reached a critical moment in his life that seemed to change everything. Like many adult learners, it took Jim a period of time to process the possibility of going back to school—weighing the pros and cons for every variable. Jim clearly displays many of the characteristics identified by Knowles as well as the importance of mattering. On the other hand, the complete transformation that is reflected in Jim's growth both as a person and learner is ultimately what makes working with adult learners so rewarding and gratifying.

Case Study: Jim

At 38, married with a three-year-old son and another child on the way, Jim had gone as far as his current position at work can possibly take him (perhaps further). As a hot baseball prospect fresh out of high school, Jim used his college experience for only one purpose: to play baseball. Of course, his poor grades eventually caught up with him at just about the same time he married his high school sweetheart at the end of his freshman year.

It was at this time that Jim dropped out of college with a less-than-impressive 1.87 GPA. School had never been a very high priority for him so he simply turned his attention to finding himself a job where he could support his new family but still provide plenty of time to play baseball. First, he took advantage of his baseball contacts to line up a job, so it was just serendipity that Jim ended up working at a home for troubled youth. When Jim was hired as a counselor, the job did not require a college degree, though later, Jim discovered he was the last person to be hired in this position without a degree. At the time, this didn't make much of an impression on Jim since he was concentrating on the single benefit of the job—his schedule, which enabled him to continue to play baseball in a semipro situation.

Since his wife, who was older than Jim, was able to obtain a position as a teacher, they were not suffering financially and Jim's concerns related more to sustaining his "career" in baseball. In fact, that might have been his legacy as he and his wife continued their life with little variation. But then about four years ago, his wife announced that she was pregnant. This is when Jim's life began to change.

After the birth of his son, everything began to look different to Jim. He had always taken his job for granted. His thinking had always been short term and so Jim had not taken much time for introspection or long-range planning. Over the years, he had seen others hired in similar jobs to his own and then advance beyond his position, but that had never seemed very important to him then. At the same time, he had always received excellent evaluations and he had always been well liked at work—it was just that his interests and priorities were elsewhere. However, being a father began to change his perspective and his desire to provide a greater level of security for his family began to take on new importance. Furthermore, it was also during this time when he first learned that no further promotions would be possible for him unless he obtained a degree.

Jim and his wife had already begun having tentative conversations about completing his education so that he could gain a promotion. Although Jim still had some qualms about going back to school, he thought he would give it a try. But then something else unexpected happened: Jim's wife announced that she was pregnant again. For Jim, this was a galvanizing moment as he envisioned himself at a crossroad and what the full implications of his decision would likely mean to the future of his family. He saw clearly that he had two options: Either he maintained the status quo where many employment opportunities would be beyond his grasp, or he completed a degree, thereby making himself much more marketable. With these implications clearly in focus, Jim was finally unequivocal about his decision. In fact, now that he had made up his mind, he felt like he had hit a home run. Once he had decided that going back to college was the sure path to success, his biggest concern was choosing a school that provided the best fit. Fortunately, a university that had a dynamic adult program was located within 15 minutes of his home and workplace. But making this decision was just the first obstacle Jim was about to encounter.

Suddenly, Jim realized that he was somewhat intimidated about going back into the classroom since he hadn't been overly successful in the past, even though Wynona, the admission counselor who worked exclusively with adult learners, kept reassuring him that his work skills and motivation served as strong predictors for his success. But while Jim acknowledged that he did indeed have a goal, he didn't feel very confident about his ability to succeed. As Jim began taking courses, he soon discovered that he was often able to draw from his experiences in the workplace to support the learning in the classroom. But eventually, Jim also realized that the experiences he was drawing upon were not just restricted to what he had gained from working with troubled youth. It was a special moment of insight when Jim fully understood that the kinds of experience he had gained from developing good work habits like being a good listener—or even from baseball—were also helpful in their classroom application. It was at this point that Jim ultimately began to really believe he had the capacity to succeed as an adult learner.

Jim recently finally completed his B. A. in sociology. Much to his surprise, he's now preparing to go to graduate school. Although he was uncertain what field to choose when he first enrolled, once he took his first sociology course, the matter was quickly settled. "I really enjoyed studying this discipline," Jim enthuses, "and the professors actually regarded my experiences at work as having value—that was really special! Furthermore, I felt like I was a particularly strong contributor when it came to classes like teambuilding or group dynamics where I could draw from all my experiences on the baseball field. Now, I find I can't get enough of learning so I'm looking forward to further studies."

Conclusion

Like many adult learners, Jim was a late entry in the pursuit of a degree. He was typical of so many of his classmates in his lack of confidence and anxiety over how well he might do. But now we can see that Jim has all the attributes that professors typically seek: He is highly motivated, he is more likely to be learning at higher levels since he is constantly making connections to previous knowledge and experiences, and he is serious about his task since he has so much at stake if he fails. But perhaps what makes Jim's story more special than anything else is his newfound enthusiasm for learning. Although his initial collegiate experience may not have been successful, he is now better able to appreciate his accomplishments since he can frame them within a more meaningful context.

● ● ● ● ●

Definition of Adult Degree Completion Program

The North Central Association's Higher Learning Commission authorized a Task Force on Adult Degree Completion Programs. The very notion that this group of 15 experts was assembled in the first place serves as a powerful testimony to the status of adult learning programs on today's campus. In their report, they offered their working definition of an adult degree completion program:

> An *adult degree completion program* is one that is designed especially to meet the needs of the working adult who, having acquired sixty or more college credit hours during previous enrollments, is returning to school after an extended period of absence to obtain a baccalaureate degree. The institution's

> promise that the student will be able to complete the program in fewer than two years of continuous study is realized through provisions such as establishing alternative class schedules, truncating the traditional semester/quarter time frame, organizing student cohorts, and awarding credit for prior learning experiences equivalent to approximately 25 percent of the bachelor's degree credit hour total. (Task Force on Adult Degree Completion Programs, 2000, p. 2)

A more detailed explication of the lessons learned from this task force are reported in Chapter 4, based on the strengths and good practices they identified in their final report.

Even though most adult learners primarily seek degree completion or certificates, they have often been treated like they are peripheral to the academy or its mission. Despite the fact that adult learners have represented a significant proportion of the total higher education enrollment since the mid-1980s, there are still only a few institutions that treat them like they are a central part of the school's mission. It is not enough to simply offer adult learner programs or courses. Colleges and universities are going to have to begin recognizing adult learners and treating them more systemically. Since these programs are expected to sustain at least 45% of the total student population well into the foreseeable future, adult learner programs are more likely to be recognized as "a functioning system of values, policies, organizations, and processes intended to provide individuals with access, opportunities, and services to support their learning" rather than merely as a "principle or organizing concept" (Maehl, 2000, p. 4).

How Adults Learn Based on Learning Theories

In an article in *The Chronicle of Higher Education,* Arthur E. Levine (2000), president of Teachers College of Columbia University, wrote about the future of colleges, where he envisions a number of inevitable changes. Although some of his vision may be speculative, there can be no doubt that when he says, "Higher education is becoming more individualized; students, not institutions, will set the educational agenda. Increasingly, students will come from diverse backgrounds and will have a widening variety of educational needs" (p. B10), the future he envisions is, at least as it applies to adult learners, already upon us. Best practices among adult learner instructors are often primarily based upon or rely heavily upon a learner-centered classroom where the instructor is mindful of the needs of the adult learner. It is therefore incumbent upon the instructor to understand those distinctive qualities that mark how an adult learns. There are a number of notable adult learning theories that have been presented during the past 25 years. Although most of these theories may be seen as competing, they are all somewhat interactive. Probably no single theory is capable of standing alone since adult learners do not fit into any single, neat category. It is evident that those practices based upon andragogy seem to serve as a strong foundation upon which other theories may be added. In large part this is because andragogy is the only adult learning theory that draws extensively from active applications rather than abstract conceptualizations. Concurrently, it is evident that andragogy is insufficient to cover all aspects of what makes adult learning unique and distinctive. It was Malcolm Knowles (1980, 1984) who emphasized that a good andragogical approach to the adult learner includes a set of assumptions. His framework includes:

1) Adults are motivated to learn by internal factors rather than those that are external. (1984, p. 12)

2) As a person matures, his or her self-concept moves from that of a dependent personality toward one of a self-directing human being.

3) An adult accumulates a growing reservoir of experience, which is a rich resource for learning.

4) The readiness of an adult to learn is closely related to the developmental tasks of his or her social role.

5) There is a change in time perspective as people mature—from future application of knowledge to immediacy of application. Thus, an adult is more problem-centered than subject-centered in learning. (1980, pp. 44–45)

Although there are many articles and chapters devoted to the topic of adult learning theory, there seems to be little agreement on a single solution. As a result, this may be one of those areas where the similarities between adult learning and jazz education (noted briefly in Chapter 1) are readily evident. While everyone can agree that jazz exists, nobody seems to be able to agree on a definition. While everyone can agree that an adult learning theory exists, nobody seems to be able to provide a fully definitive example. Regardless of whether there is agreement or not, successful instructors for adult learners will strive to understand how their students are learning and modify their instruction accordingly. After all, theory evolves out of practice.

Experiential Learning: The Foundation for Adult Learning

Perhaps the best illustration of this concept is expressed in the term "experiential learning." Note how this theme is woven throughout the various aspects of learning theory and concepts focusing on the adult learner. In 1994, the unifying framework behind the International Experiential Learning Conference was based on the belief in and the practice of experiential learning, which, for adults, goes beyond reading and listening as the primary routes to effective learning. Sheckley and Weil (1994) demonstrate how the interplay between assimilation and accommodation contributes to adult learning in the realm of formal operational thought:

> Experiential learning practitioners know the pitfalls of an educational program biased toward assimilation and the use of formal operational thought. First, an overemphasis on assimilation can limit the learning process. When assimilation dominates over accommodation the learner actively adds to the abstract models he/she uses to understand and represent the world but the abstractions that are assimilated have few affective or personal components. Consider a learner who dutifully uses formal operations to memorize (assimilate) formulae for chemistry courses only to parrot the information back on semester examinations. If this learner never accommodates any of the assimilated facts about chemistry to his/her day-to-day experiences, facts about chemistry are just sterile answers to exam questions.
>
> Second, and more importantly, if accommodation is not included in the learning process, there is no possible way a learner can verify the meaning of assimilated concepts. An abstract proposition is equivalent to a list of *"if... then..."* statements in which the *"if"* clause refers to what we would then experience if the abstract proposition is true. If abstract concepts are only assimilated and never tested out in experience (accommodated), their truth [*sic*] value goes untested. (p. 9)

These observations are at the very core of how adults are likely to approach their learning. All lessons resonate best among adult learners when they are able to experience the learning and demonstrate how what they have learned can be shown to be relevant.

But perhaps a more specific illustration will provide even greater insight into this concept. In a booklet titled *Learning is About Making Connections,* Cross (1999), citing the research of deGroot (1966), illustrates the importance of prior knowledge and experiential learning.

> Chess players of different skill levels were shown the game pieces on a chessboard for a few seconds and then asked to recall the position of the pieces. The novice players were able to place only five or six pieces correctly, but the experts could recreate nearly the whole board. However, when these players were shown the pieces placed randomly on the board (rather than positions from a real game), novices and experts performed about the same. The conclusion from this rather simple experiment is that the superior performance of experienced chess players in recalling chess positions was not due to higher IQs or to better memories, but rather to a schema for chess that enabled experienced players to associate the patterns shown with those already in memory. The point is that what one knows about a given subject has a substantial impact on the learning process. When teachers complain that students can't read, they are pointing not only to the lack of reading skills, but also the density of the schema for a particular subject matter. For example, I am a "better reader" in psychology than in economics because I have a well-developed schema for the terms, concepts, and even the "ways of thinking" of psychologists. (p. 10)

Cross later reminds us that it is John Dewey who is the father of experiential learning as she continues to illustrate the various connections between formal schooling and experience.

The Need for Instructional Diversity

When working with adult learners, the successful instructor quickly understands the need to employ diverse strategies and activities for the classroom. Because so many of the adult courses are in an accelerated format, instructors cannot simply afford to "talk faster." In fact, the first transformation required for successful adult instruction is based on abandoning the lecture format for more action- or application-based learning experiences. Furthermore (especially in the accelerated format), although the outcomes are expected to concur with those courses that feature greater seat time, the proportions of time and workload efforts require a fresh approach for those instructors unfamiliar with this format. Advance assignments, substitutes for tests, study groups that complete much of the work outside the classroom, and self-directed learning are all features of this new paradigm. Clearly, any instructor who is unwilling to adapt a different instructional strategy for the adult learner classroom will encounter serious problems. Instead, successful models tend to employ a level of flexibility and sensitivity to the needs of the learners that one seldom encounters in more conventional classroom settings.

Conclusion

The 21st century is very likely to become a sea change in the history of the academy. In part, of course, this dramatic shift will be attributable to technology, a focal point for most of the visionary leaders, authors, and researchers in higher education today. Adult learners are much less likely to be recognized as a prominent change factor for the 21st century, even though their numbers already are close to 50% of the total student population. However, the characteristics that define adult learners are more likely to define all students in 21st century higher education, primarily because the lines between student types show some signs of blurring and many younger students are exhibiting behaviors and characteristics previously attributed to their older classmates. In part, this may be attributable to technology both in the classroom and in the way it affects our lives. Furthermore, as indicated in the previous chapter, the practices and strategies that have been employed among successful adult programs are also likely to define and influence institutions in the future as well. Of course, visionary institutions that have achieved appreciation for and understanding of the best practices associated with adult learner programs are likely to enjoy a significant advantage in this change climate.

In my capacity as Dean of Lifelong Learning, nearly 50% of the student-faculty conflicts I encounter are a result of the instructor's insensitivity to the adult learner as a phenomenon. When professors assume they can treat their adult learners the same as their younger classmates, or when they approach the classroom with a rigid perspective that doesn't take into account any of the challenges or extra responsibilities adult learners are likely to bring into the classroom, they do nothing to maximize the situation. All too often, as I begin my discussion with the instructor, he or she seems to assume that I am seeking special consideration or treatment on behalf of the adult learner. Not only is that erroneous, but in my experience, the vast majority of adult learners are seeking neither. They simply want the instructor to be mindful of and understand that their lives are filled with many responsibilities and obligations that are typically beyond the range of options for the majority of traditional-aged students. As such, they simply want the material presented and the work expected framed in such a manner that will optimize the use of whatever time they have available. In other words, they want the opportunity to demonstrate their proficiency and knowledge, even though they may have to accomplish this differently than their traditional-aged classmates.

References

Carlson, R. (1989, Spring). Malcolm Knowles: Apostle of andragogy. *Vitae Scholasticae, 8,* 1.

Commission for a Nation of Lifelong Learners. (1997). *A nation learning: Vision for the 21st century.* Albany, NY: Regents College.

Cross, K. P. (1999). *Learning is about making connections.* Mission Viejo, CA: League for Innovation in the Community College.

deGroot, A. (1966). Perception and memory versus thought: Some old ideas and recent finds. In B. Kleinmuntz (Ed.), *Problem solving.* New York, NY: John Wiley.

Knowles, M. S. (1980). *The modern practice of adult education: From pedagogy to andragogy.* New York, NY: Cambridge Books.

Knowles, M. S. (1984). *Andragogy in action: Applying modern principles of adult learning.* San Francisco, CA: Jossey-Bass.

Levine, A. E. (2000, October). The future of colleges: Nine inevitable changes. *The Chronicle of Higher Education,* pp. B10–B11.

Maehl, W. H. (2000). *Lifelong learning at its best: Innovative practices in adult credit programs.* San Francisco, CA: Jossey-Bass.

Ross-Gordon, J. (2002, Spring). Effective teaching of adults: Themes and conclusions. *New Directions for Adult and Continuing Education, 93,* 85–91.

Schlossberg, N. K., Lynch, A. Q., & Chickering, A. W. (1989). *Improving higher education environments for adults: Responsive programs and services from entry to departure.* San Francisco, CA: Jossey-Bass.

Sheckley, B. G., & Weil, S. W. (1994). Using experience to enhance learning: Perspectives and questions. In M. T. Keeton (Ed.), *Perspectives on experiential learning: Prelude to a global conversation about learning* (pp. 7–12). Chicago, IL: Council for Adult Experiential Learning.

Task Force on Adult Degree Completion Programs. (2000, June). *Adult degree completion programs.* Retrieved June 5, 2001, from http://www.ncacihe.org/resources/adctf/ADCPRept.pdf

Whitehead, A. N. (1929). *The aims of education and other essays.* New York, NY: Macmillan.

Appendix 2.1

Comparison Between Traditional Learners and Adult Learners

Traditional Learner	Adult Learner
The Learner	
Dependent personality Teacher is fully responsible for (what, how, when, whether)	Self-directed learning Anxious to learning demonstrate they are taking responsibility for themselves
The Learner's Experience	
Little *valuable* experience; relies on transmission techniques—lectures, readings, and audiovisuals	Assumes greater volume and different quality (since adults perform different roles than younger people)
Readiness to Learn	
Students become ready to learn what they are told they have to learn	Students become ready when they experience a need to know or do something
Orientation to Learning	
Subject-centered: learning as a process of acquiring prescribed subject matter content	Life-centered, task-centered, or problem-centered orientation (curriculum should focus on life situations rather than subject matter units)
Motivation to Learn	
External: pressures come from parents or teachers	Internal: self-esteem, recognition, better quality of life, greater self-confidence

[Based on Knowles, 1984]

3

Demographics and Projections

Overview

One of the characteristics that already marks the 21st century as notable is the institutional reliance on statistics and data of all sorts. The academy relies heavily on this information in order to make informed decisions and to better understand our circumstances. These objectives define the purpose of this chapter. In particular, it looks at how current figures regarding adult learners may differ from previous decades and what projections or trends are likely to characterize the future of adult learners and how that might affect the academy.

Probably the most dynamic statistic concerning adult learners in the early 21st century is the proportion of total students they represent within all of higher education: Over 47% of all students enrolled in colleges and universities today are 25 or older. But other data, such as their entering age, the changing gender proportion, as well as new delivery systems and formats that are attracting groups of students who might have been ignored in the past, all serve to remind us that this population is dynamic and often centrally involved in the dramatic changes taking place on the campus today.

Historically, adult learners have represented a small but growing portion of the total college enrollment in every decade since 1950. However, these students have seldom garnered much attention from most of the members of the academy. Since the post-WWII era, when adult learners first appeared on many campuses, adult learners have come to characterize a significant segment of the student body. Understanding this significance may provide greater insights regarding the role and importance of adult learners for the 21st century.

In fact, by the year 2005, many demographers suggest that more than 50% of all students enrolled in higher education will be 25 or older. This further suggests the likelihood that adult learning may have some notable implications in portions of higher education not even considered by most leaders at this time.

Facts and Figures

Educators have long relied on the use of statistics and demographics to provide clearer pictures of their constituents as well as to identify future trends. According to Kipp (as cited in Swail, 2002):

> Higher education is also going through significant changes stimulated by the rapid growth of the Internet, the increasing globalization of higher education, and the ever-pressing question of institutional and instructional quality. New modes of educational delivery through virtual networks are breaking the traditional mold of instructional provision. New players, new pedagogies, and new paradigms are redefining higher education. The rules are changing and there is increased pressure on institutions of higher education to evolve, adapt, or desist. (p. 16)

The first, and perhaps most stunning statistic relating to today's adult learners (most schools define this population as post-24 or post-25 in age), is that they currently represent more than 47% of all students enrolled in higher education. Although this statistic often seems to be overlooked or dismissed by many faculty and administrators who may not see how they are directly affected by its implications, there are many permutations that are likely to affect every campus in the future. Furthermore, this figure becomes even more potent since it is actually part of a longstanding and ongoing trend: that is, according to some projections, adult learners are expected to comprise more than 50% of the total enrollment in higher education by the year 2005. However, from current information supplied by the US Department of Education, National Center for Education Statistics (2002), we are also able to discern many other salient facts about today's adult learner and his or her role in higher education:

- More than 35% of all undergraduate students are represented in the current population of adult learners.
- Four-year colleges enroll about two-thirds of adult undergraduates between 25 and 34 years of age while about half of all adult undergraduates age 35 and older attend these institutions.
- For students 25 to 29 years of age, school enrollment rates have almost quadrupled since 1950 with 11.4% of this total population demographic currently enrolled in higher education.
- The figure for this demographic is even more significant when gender is considered. Enrollment rates for women 25 to 29 increased from 0.4% in 1950 to 12.7% in 2000 while men of the same age increased their enrollment rates by only 4.1% during the same period.
- For students 30 to 34 years of age, the growth enrollment rates are even more dramatic. While 1.1% of this population was enrolled in 1952, the figure for the year 2000 is 6.7%—a six-fold growth during this 50-year period.
- Once again, the rate of increase for women in this group is especially impressive. The enrollment rate for women 30 to 34 years of age grew from 0.7% in 1952 to 7.7% in 2000—an eleven-fold increase—while the rate for men of the same age only expanded 3.9% during the same period.
- In fact, women comprise the largest portion of all adult learners and do so by a significant amount: approximately 70% of all adult students are female. (p. 26)

Since women now represent an especially large portion of the adult student population, their majority often forces new or different group dynamics and group interactions to take place in the classroom. Many instructors already report that classes where the gender distribution is predominantly female are likely to interact and behave differently from those where males are in the majority. In fact, this is a perfect illustration of how adult learners provide a prototype for the academy: In 1996, women students of all ages comprised 56% of all college students—in large part due to the high distribution of adult women learners (46% of all women enrolled in college were 25 or older). While the portion of adult female students is expected to decline to 41% of all women enrolled in college through 2008, female students are projected to comprise 57% of the total enrollment so that numbers are expected to increase in all age brackets for women. This trend suggests that many classrooms for traditional students are also likely to become female dominant in the future, based on gender distribution. Here's an opportunity for instructors who may normally only teach 18- to 22-year-old students to learn from the experiences of their colleagues teaching adult learners since many more will have already experienced this phenomenon.

Furthermore, because many of the adult learner demographics seem to anticipate the academy of the future, other lessons learned from working with adults may especially lend themselves to future applications for all students. Here are more statistics that help define the 21st century adult learner:

- The typical adult learner enrolled in schools today has a family income of approximately $50,000.
- Undergraduate enrollment status (i.e., part-time or full-time) is strongly related to age—full-time enrollment decreases as each age bracket increases. For instance, although approximately 51% of students in the 25 to 29 age bracket have full-time status, only approximately 39% of students in the 30 to 34 range are full-time. This number continues to decline as age increases.
- Almost 70% of all adult undergraduate learners overall are registered part-time—the majority of them typically taking one course at a time. ("One course at a time," however, may be, in part, skewed data as a result of the high proportion of adult students enrolled in cohort programs that are designed to only utilize one course at any time.)
- While the median age for undergraduate adult learners is almost 38 years, more than 45% of these students are 40 or older.
- In excess of 65% of these students are married.
- Approximately 70% are seeking a degree (as opposed to a certificate or simply studying for the sake of learning).

- The vast majority of adults (especially when those who select the certificate option are factored in) are pursuing professional studies, particularly in business, health, or education.
- A trend that clearly reflects today's changing lifestyle is that approximately 90% of adult students have access to a computer—either at home or at the workplace.
- Almost 80% of adult learners are employed. However, the uncertainty associated with the job marketplace (e.g., downsizing, cutbacks, or technological advances) may be one of the major driving forces behind the continuing increase of adult student enrollment.
- Only 21% of American adults over the age of 25 have a bachelor's degree or better!

Financial Motivation

Although there are a number of factors that motivate adults to enroll in college, the financial benefits associated with obtaining a degree are clearly one of the more significant. In fact, according to the US Census Bureau, as cited in *Postsecondary Education Opportunity* (Mortenson Research Seminar on Public Policy Analysis, 2001), the average family income, based on educational attainment of the householder, shows the widest gap between those who possess "some college" or an "associate's degree" and those who possess a "bachelor's degree" (see Figure 3.1).

FIGURE 3.1

Average Family Income

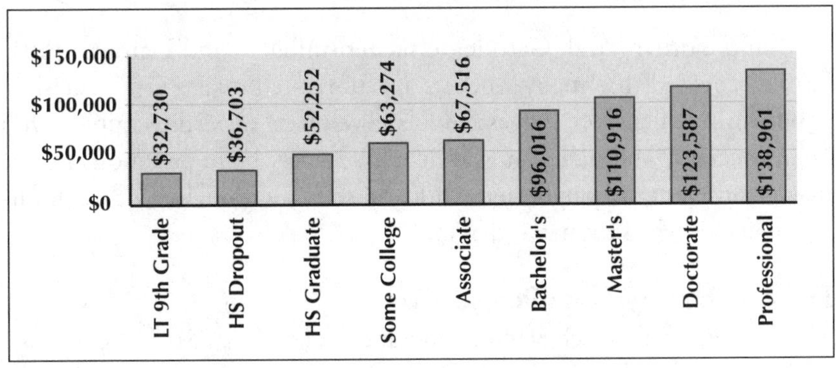

The Knowledge Web (2000) reported these data from a different perspective when they indicated that in 1980 the salary gap between high school and college graduates was 50%, but in 2000 that gap had skyrocketed to 111%! This certainly suggests that the "marketability" of a degree in today's world has credence. Another perspective may provide even more evidence regarding the compelling relationship between income and education. Between 1970 and 2000, the level of educational attainment in the civil labor force increased significantly—signaling the importance of attaining as much education as possible. While that portion of the labor force with a high school diploma or less declined in numbers during this period, those workers with some college or a degree dramatically increased. Specific levels indicate the following:

- The share of the labor force lacking a high school diploma has been reduced from 36.1% to 9.8% during the past 30 years.
- Those workers who only possess a high school diploma or GED decreased from 38.1% to 31.8%.
- Workers with some college or an associate degree increased from 11.8% to 27.9% since 1970.
- The share of the labor force who at least achieved a bachelor's degree increased from 14.1% to 30.4%.
- More than two-thirds of workers in growing, good-paying occupations have postsecondary education.
- 87% of "elite job" holders and 53% of "good job" holders have more than a high school education.

On the other hand, Gardner, Csikszentmihalyi, and Damon (2001) have discovered that many workers are motivated by a desire to achieve good work, which they suggest entails developing expertise coupled with helping society. As such, some adult learners may be highly motivated to make a difference through their work and they are more likely to seek further education as a means to that end.

From a State-by-State Perspective

The Mortenson Research Seminar on Public Policy Analysis of Opportunity for Postsecondary Education joined the Council for Adult and Experiential

Learning (CAEL) to investigate enrollment rates by state for adult undergraduates as well as by gender and age groups. Although their full report may be obtained as a large Excel workbook at www.postsecondary.org, according to the November 2001 issue of *Postsecondary Education Opportunity*, the most notable patterns confirmed that:

- The 13 states with the highest enrollment rates for undergraduates are all western states.
- The states with the lowest enrollment rates are all New England or mid-Atlantic states.

This report indicates that the range of scores among all but 10% of the states is very narrow. The more extreme enrollment rates (i.e., very high or very low), however, are centered upon western, New England, or mid-Atlantic states, thus producing the results noted above. Nonetheless, the statistics derived from this study do provide a clearer picture of the enrollment patterns of adults by state, which may be helpful when trying to determine regional trends or obtaining regional perspectives.

Not All Adult Learners Are in Their 20s or 30s

Adult learners are a perfect demographic to demonstrate the "graying of America" phenomenon. Here's one final demographic set of data about adult learners to consider:

- In 1935, when Social Security was first established in the United States, age 65 typically represented the end of life expectancy. In the 21st century, an average 65-year-old person can look forward to more than 20 years of a significantly more active and engaged lifestyle than his or her predecessors. Learning—at one level of involvement or another—has become much more important among the members of this demographic group.
- In 1987, for the first time ever, Americans over the age of 65 outnumbered those under 25.
- In the year 2001, the largest age group was 30 to 44, with a steeply rising curve for 45- to 65-year-olds.
- As a result, within the next ten years, Americans over the age of 65 will represent the largest single demographic—by far!

- More than 80% of today's 20-year-olds have completed four years of high school compared with less than half of those in their grandparents' generation. (Since previous education is the single best predictor of participation in adult education, the rising educational level of the adult population is a significant contextual factor. While this generation may not appear among current enrollment patterns for adult learners, there is a greater likelihood that they will, sometime in their lives, enroll as an adult learner—swelling the figures even more.)

New Delivery Systems

Statistics and demographics need not be restricted to just the students. In the past 50 years, there have been a number of institutional responses to the adult learner. Although the majority of these initiatives have been generated from within the academy, the amount of growth among for-profit, virtual, and corporate entities is astonishing.

- In 2002, the University of Phoenix, part of the Apollo Group, saw its enrollment surpass 100,000 students—making it the largest institution of higher learning in the United States.
- In October 1999, Newman noted, "Over two hundred for-profit colleges and universities have entered our world, and more are coming" (p. 1).
- Degree-granting for-profit two-year institutions rose 78%, to 483, from 1989 to 1999. During that same period the number of public two-year institutions grew 9%, to 1,075.
- For-profit four-year degree-granting colleges showed even more growth. From 1989 to 1999, they showed an increase of 266%, to 194. That number continues to grow. In comparison, public institutions grew 3%, to 613 schools. The number of private colleges increased 4%, to 1,536.
- Corporate universities have exploded in terms of the number of companies who have integrated some formal learning system into their makeup—especially in the past ten years as more corporations have moved beyond the campus concept (where the focus is on the physical) to a corporate process that links training to the organization's competitive advantage.

Meister (1994) identifies six skills—learning skills, basic skills, interpersonal skills, creative-thinking skills, leadership skills, and self-management skills—as well as the scope and mission of Corporate Quality Universities to include:

- Building a competency-based training curriculum for each job classification.
- Providing all levels of employees with a common shared vision of the company and its values and culture.
- Extending training to the company's entire customer/supply chain, including customers, suppliers, and even the universities that supply the company with its human talent (i.e., the company's new hires).
- Serving as a learning laboratory for experimenting with new approaches and practices for the design and delivery of both formal and informal learning initiatives. (p. 23)

While the scope, mission, and skills identified here relate closely to those found at many colleges or universities, the similarity doesn't stop there: These programs also emphasize promoting a spirit of lifelong learning as an integral part of their philosophy. In short, these institutions contribute to the blurring of lines between themselves and traditional colleges and universities.

But perhaps the most notable development relates to the use of technology, particularly as it is used for online instruction. Although this field is still in its infancy, certain best practices have already been identified and disseminated. These include 1) skill development embedded in the context of interest to the learner and a primary focus on active learning, and 2) a commitment to emphasis on the learning rather than on the technology.

- Our economy is no longer centered on a manufacturing base, but rather depends largely on "knowledge workers." Since 1950, employment in the manufacturing sector has fallen from nearly 40% of total employment to less than 18% today while service sector employment (comprised of highly skilled workers) has risen from less than 14% to more than 35%.

- Success in these industries is primarily reliant on how companies obtain, train, and retain these workers. In 2000, companies devoted over $9.4 billion to online learning initiatives. By the year 2003, the estimated expenditure for this area is projected to grow to $53.3 billion.
- Colleges and universities offer greater access to the web than any other entity, with over 90% of all college students accessing the Internet, 52% of them daily.
- More than 2.2 million college students were expected to enroll in online distributed courses in 2002, up from 710,000 in 1998—a threefold increase.
- The number of US households online was projected to grow from nearly 30 million in 1998 to nearly 70 million by the end of 2002, when 90% of homes were expected to have PCs and 64% were expected to be online.

At this point, a prototype of the typical adult learner should be evident to the reader as well as the sorts of learning and learning environments he or she is most likely to encounter. To better illustrate this prototype, the next case study offers a composite of the "typical" adult learner in the 21st century. Not only does this student fit the profile regarding her age, gender, and experience, but her goals are similar, and she has even taken some online instruction in order to complete her studies. Furthermore, like so many of her peers, she has already determined that she wants more education—it's just a matter of how much!

In many ways, Marjorie typifies the adult learner today. With two of her children in high school and two in college, she has finally managed to position herself so that she can complete her own schooling. Having helped to support her family for the past 20 years, she is now enrolled in a degree completion program that will position her to start a whole new career at the age of 42. Marjorie figures she has at least 20 years to establish a career of her own and it's that vision that has kept her motivated every day of her college studies.

Case Study: Marjorie

Marjorie began college as a typical 18-year-old, but within two years she was married and pregnant. Since her husband needed to complete his education, they decided that she would leave school to raise the family and work as much as possible to help make ends meet. It was only much later, when the fourth and final child was in high school (and with two of her children already in college) that she finally had the opportunity to once again become a college student herself.

It was during the time she was getting George, her second son, settled into college that she picked up some literature from his school's Lifelong Learning Center. Driving home, all she could think about was the instant image she got when she quickly scanned that pamphlet: She saw herself as a successful businesswoman, running her own company. When she got back to work on Monday, she confirmed that her company provided tuition reimbursement, which was, for her, the final deciding factor. Without some support from her workplace, the financial demands for tuition, books, etc. probably would have been impossible at this time. But now she felt she was in the right position to take advantage of this opportunity. Although going to school was obviously going to take up a lot of her time, she felt she now had some to spare since both of her sons were already in college. Within a month, she was enrolled for her first two courses.

Marjorie was delighted to work closely with Suzanne, her advisor at the school. Together, they were able to determine just how long it would take Marjorie to complete her studies since the program for adults published a two-year schedule, outlining all courses to be offered to the adult learners during that period. It was at Marjorie's second advising session that she and Suzanne were able to carefully plot Marjorie's entire sequence of courses—when and how she would be able to complete them. Because the school also offered a diverse set of options regarding the various days, times, and formats that the courses could be taken, Suzanne was able to show Marjorie how she could combine semester-long courses with more accelerated courses to finish as quickly as possible without overburdening herself too much. Furthermore, Marjorie was also able to take advantage of three distance-learning courses that she managed to fit into her schedule during breaks between semesters.

Suzanne was also helpful in providing noncurricular information as well. For instance, she recommended that Marjorie needed to work closely with her husband and two daughters still at home in order to help them understand about her decision to return to school. Suzanne pointed out that adult learners often encountered problems at home when they weren't able to articulate the reasons for going to school. She also suggested that having their support could substantially help her during this period when every minute was critical. "Too many adult students never articulate why they are seeking to complete their degree or even talk about the help they may need to their loved ones," Suzanne explained. "Help them to understand your needs for their support and assistance but also take a moment to share your vision."

Marjorie quickly came to rely on Suzanne as her advocate, but she was still startled during the summer at the end of her first year of study when Suzanne contacted her to suggest she consider modifying her long-range schedule only slightly to accommodate taking some courses that not only satisfied her degree completion work but could also be applied toward a master's degree as well.

"I've been so focused on getting my degree that I never thought beyond it," Marjorie told Suzanne. But it didn't take her long to realize that, given her ambitions, an undergraduate degree probably wasn't going to be sufficient for her. Since beginning her studies again she was consumed with the idea of running her own business. Although Suzanne was the only person other than her family that Marjorie had shared this dream with, she was now especially pleased that she had someone like Suzanne she could trust at the school, as she quickly realized what a wise option the further degree posed for her.

And so, when Marjorie was ready to graduate, it was fitting that she asked Suzanne to be her sponsor in the precommencement ceremony for adult students. The graduates were asked to identify the one special person who had been particularly helpful and instrumental in assisting them to reach this point in their life. "Not only was Suzanne a great advisor in helping strategize how I could complete my degree, she was a constant source of information and support that made all the difference in the quality of my experience at the school. She was great!"

Conclusion

Like so many adult learners, Marjorie never lacked the intellectual skills and equipment to be a successful college student, she simply needed the opportunity. Fortunately for her, she was able to complete her degree in time to begin a new career. But perhaps even more telling, with the help of a good advisor (research suggests that good advising support may be the single most critical factor in defining quality adult learning programs), she was able to enlist her family to "buy in" to her vision and plan well in advance so that she had a clear sense of what her task entailed. When Marjorie encountered an extra opportunity (the additional degree), she was able to manage it because she had a clear notion of the options, and felt she could make an informed decision. Support, clarity, planning, viable options, and clearly defined objectives—these are the very attributes that tend to define successful adult learner experiences.

● ● ● ● ●

Another Way of Thinking About Diversity

We have seen a greater emphasis placed on the issue of "diversity" at almost all schools. Although the term is ambiguous enough to enable schools to decide for themselves what constitutes a diverse population, the notion of age being one facet of diversity seldom receives any attention or consideration as a variable for inclusion. Many astute authors have emphasized that our culture has been youth-oriented for many years. Nonetheless, schools who are seeking broader ways of thinking about diversity would be well served to be more intentional about including students of all ages and identifying ways to better serve the needs of their adult learners.

Indeed, the most overlooked segment of adult learners may be that group at or near retirement. Because our culture has seldom embraced the senior citizen as a rich resource for our own learning, most institutions have also marginalized them when it comes to learning opportunities. However, while the options for learning among the retired may be somewhat limited, and even though schools may not be spending much time or effort in expanding on those options, their immense numbers are going to start forcing schools to pay more attention.

Any person who expects to have 20 years left for a career is likely to gain the attention of adult learning programs in most places. That, however, has not been the case when it comes to senior citizens, even though it is inevitable that more of them (simply by dint of their numbers) are going to be seeking new credentials with a new career in mind. After all, not everybody wants to simply retire or play golf. It is therefore very evident that a growing number of older students will be seeking either degree completion or certificates through adult learning programs.

THE 21ST CENTURY ACADEMY

Despite the paucity of statistics, there is ample anecdotal evidence already in place to suggest that the academy of the 21st century is likely to change more than ever in its entire history. In part, today's traditional students will force that change. Because the younger generation has had greater exposure to a technological environment that many college professors still grapple with (and some even disdain) and because these same students have often been engaged in learning situations that rely heavily on that technology throughout their entire K–12 experience, they and future generations bring new orientations and expectations to their college experience that differ significantly from any previous set of students. One additional significant factor is the future job market. By 2008, it is estimated that more than 14 million new jobs requiring some postsecondary education or at least a bachelor's degree will be created. This number more than doubles those jobs expected to be created that will require high school level skills or below. But there are a few statistics that emphasize how today's 18- to 22-year-olds are experiencing a dramatically different kind of collegiate experience than previous generations. What makes these data even more notable is how they reflect greater similarities between the adult learner and 18- to 22-year-old students.

- Course load averages are 13 to 14 hours per semester.
- More than 70% of these students work an average of 37 hours per week.
- They experience higher levels of stress than preceding generations.
- More than 75% report they have done volunteer work (i.e., active, service learning).

- They describe themselves as consumer oriented, pragmatic, career oriented, and committed to doing well in the classroom.

These items suggest that the differences between adult learners and 18- to 22-year-olds are narrowing or blurring to an extent that is likely to change the complexion on the campus of the future. Specifically, accelerated courses, specialized schedules with times appropriate for pre- or post-work learning opportunities, and other delivery systems that have often been restricted to adult learners are more likely to be extended to all students in the future. Likewise, many of the attitudes and objectives cited as unique among adult learners are now beginning to emerge as congruent with traditional students as well.

The "New" 18- to 22-Year-Old Student

A new trend has begun to emerge and be recognized at many schools relating to a new type of student. Although they may not represent a significant number of students today, they have begun to emerge in sufficient numbers to warrant their recognition in conversations among leaders in adult education. Typically, this student is extremely savvy when it comes to technology (many students in this category begin working for technology as early as the summer between their sophomore and junior year in high school). As soon as they graduate from high school, they are already in great demand—often being hired in a middle management position where they are in charge of a number of adults who don't have as much knowledge about technology as this 18-year-old possesses. But because these students have already been working summers and/or part-time with these companies, they usually display a level of maturity that belies their years.

The next phase happens once the young person settles into a position to the point he or she is comfortable with the workload. At that point, this individual is likely to seek admission to a college or university as an adult learner (despite their age). Because the student to be is working full-time (more typically, over 50 hours a week), because he or she usually has some sort of supervisory position managing many older adults, and because this person tends to be much more mature than his or her peers, it is hard to imagine them being anything but an adult student. But it does call into question how to best define an adult learner and it certainly suggests that some of the distinguishing factors may be more blurred in the future.

Even When They're Substantial, Sometimes Numbers Don't Count

As enrollment figures for adult learners continue to increase, there is some evidence that adult learning programs at many schools receive the Rodney Dangerfield treatment: That is, they don't get any respect. Although there are a number of contributing factors for this phenomenon—many of which are discussed throughout this book—a lot comes down to how adult programs have long been marginalized rather than mainstreamed into the campus culture. The programs have had to be flexible and resilient just to survive. In fact, they have been in a constant state of transformation for the past 50 years, in some ways reinventing themselves repeatedly. For many faculty and administrators, the constant change and entrepreneurial response associated with it may have posed a serious challenge, since the academy has largely been about maintaining the status quo. For instance, on many campuses adult learners find that support systems, curricular consideration, or sensitivity to their special learning needs may not be provided to the extent enjoyed by their daytime classmates. The conversation at faculty meetings, institutes, or conferences seldom turns to any aspect or consideration of the adult learner on campus (unless, of course, the topic is specifically adult learner related). Therefore, we can't simply rely on statistics in order to understand the adult program phenomenon. In addition, the admissions criterion reference to "post-25" used by many schools often tends to obscure the accurate picture of adult students as well. That is, while the qualifying age for adult learners may indeed be 25 or older, the average enrollment age at the national level is now slightly more than 40 years. This statistic matches "the graying of America" phenomenon cited by many demographers (that is, as a nation we are growing older) but it also tends to further confuse the issue in the minds of those individuals in the academy who may wish to pigeonhole or solidify any characteristics of the adult learner in their mind.

The inability of many faculty members to respond to this large segment of the student population is at the heart of the internal struggle for identity and mission on many campuses. Nonetheless, as the statistics clearly imply, adult learners represent a dynamic and growing portion of the student population that will ultimately and inevitably lead to a sea change in the academy during this century. Fundamentally, most professors at four-year institutions, as well as many administrators who lead these institutions, came through a system themselves—and largely envision its continuation—where the 18- to 22-year-old student is the focal point for undergraduate education. But as we shall see in upcoming chapters, adult students bring an entirely different set of expectations into the classroom than traditional students. In turn, these issues are often at the root of the dichotomy between instructors who prefer one student type above the other. One fundamental premise of this book, however, is that success with these populations need not be mutually exclusive. Consequently, as this book continues to explore the differences between these populations, the reader is urged to remain sensitive to the notable demographics that convey how many adult learners will populate higher education today and in the future.

Conclusion

Having a comprehensive understanding of what comprises the typical adult learner can be very helpful for any instructor or administrator working with him or her, especially if one is willing to treat this population with respect. Adult learners have grown in number to the point that they represent half of all students enrolled in higher education. But the response from higher education has not always reflected proportionate or appropriate reactions to such a dominant population. Often, a lack of understanding or respect toward the adult learner has proven to be the weakest link in attracting and/or retaining them as students. Very few schools can afford to ignore what is likely to be the majority of their future student body, and smart schools will want to learn how to attract the best of this population.

In many ways, today's students, regardless of whether they are traditional or adult, will be recycled in the future—probably on more than one occasion. For centuries, the academy has perceived that an advanced degree is the appropriate response to undergraduates seeking further education. Today, that may no longer be the case. While many professions are likely to call for advanced degrees as a point of entry, there is likely to be increasing emphasis on the continuation of knowledge as a critical factor for sustaining and improving any person's credentials. If that is indeed true, successful adult learning programs are likely to play an even greater role in the academy of the future. At any rate, adult learners are likely to continue to influence changes in the academy of the future.

Even as the enrollment numbers and proportion of overall student population increase and factors relating to curriculum, instruction, technology, and scheduling that have been designed to meet the needs of adult learners continue to influence the very nature of the academy, greater attention will inevitably focus on how to utilize the best of these practices across the entire student population. For instance, there is already greater use of distance education for all student populations than ever before, though the roots of these formats are largely derivative of adult programs (see Chapter 10). The lessons learned among many of the most successful adult learner programs are easily accessible for those schools seeking innovative yet proven solutions to the new challenges that face the academy in the 21st century.

The figures cited in this chapter can be powerful reminders of how dramatically things are changing in higher education. Occasionally, I will have a discussion with a group of faculty members who are very resistant to the whole concept of adult learners. I have encountered some faculty members who seem to be in denial about the statistics cited here. It is easy to ignore a significant and growing population if you don't have any direct interaction with them, especially if you believe that they are not the population you wish to serve in the first place. But this is a position that fewer faculty members can afford to hold in the future. Like it or not, teaching on almost any college campus will entail teaching some adult learners as the century progresses. But some faculty members seem to have a narrow notion of the students they seek to interact with and tend to dismiss all other students who don't fall in this a priori category.

For instance, I had an opportunity to speak before a school's faculty at a conference that had been set up to begin the semester. One of the main points in my presentation was to put adult learners into perspective, based on demographic information and projections. The school already had an adult program that had been in existence for a number of years and had enjoyed a solid reputation. Adult learners comprised approximately 30% of the undergraduate student population at this school and about 90% of the modest graduate program the school offered. When I completed my presentation, there was a series of questions regarding the demographic information I had shared. "How many of these adults are at community colleges?" was the first question an eager faculty member asked. When I indicated that a substantial portion of adult learners are enrolled at community colleges, it was obvious that some of the faculty members were ready to believe that they were therefore exempt from having to further consider adult learners. However, when I pointed out that the vast majority of adult students who came to their school or any other four-year school were likely to complete the first two years of learning at a community college prior to degree completion, some of them began to understand the full implications. Unfortunately, however, a few of the faculty members made it clear that they were only concerned with traditional students and discussion about any other group was "not part of their domain." When I suggested that even some traditional students were beginning to assume portions of the demeanor and attitudes expressed by typical adult learners, the response was, "If it's been good enough for the academy during the past few centuries, it's good enough for these students." Well, maybe—but I wouldn't have written this book if I believed that were true.

References

Aslanian, C. (2001). *Adult students today.* Washington, DC: The College Board.

Gardner, H., Csikszentmihalyi, M., & Damon, W. (2001). *Good work: When excellence and ethics meet.* New York, NY: Basic Books.

Kipp, S. M. (1998). Demographic trends and their impact on the future of the Pell grant program. In L. E. Gladieux, B. Astor, & W. S. Swail (Eds.), *Memory, reason, and imagination: A quarter century of Pell grants* (p. 109). New York, NY: The College Board.

Meister, J. C. (1994). *Corporate quality universities: Lessons in building a world-class work force.* Chicago, IL: Irwin Professional Publishing.

Moe, M. T., & Blodget, H. (2000). *The knowledge web.* New York, NY: Merrill Lynch & Co.

Mortenson Research Seminar on Public Policy Analysis. (2001, November). *Postsecondary education opportunity.* Oskaloosa, IA: Author.

Mortenson Research Seminar on Public Policy Analysis. (2001, December). *Postsecondary education opportunity.* Oskaloosa, IA: Author.

Newman, F. (1999, October 12). *Intellectual skills in the information age.* Retrieved August 22, 2001, from http://www.futuresproject.org/publications/intellectual_skills.pdf

Swail, W. S. (2002, July/August). Higher education and the new demographics: Questions for policy. *Change,* 15–23.

US Department of Education, National Center for Education Statistics. (2002). *The condition of education 2002* (NCES 2002-025). Washington, DC: Author.

4
Programmatic Best Practices

Overview

As the enrollment of adult learners continues to grow, the number and variety of programs designed to explicitly serve this population has expanded as well. During the past 20 years, as the rate of growth has accelerated, the issue of quality associated with these programs has also taken on greater significance. While some of the programs may have posed special qualitative challenges based on their design, expectations, or pedagogical practices, these shortcomings have often helped organizations devoted to adult learner issues focus on what constitutes best practices. At a time when assessment has become one of the primary factors in supporting or defining accreditation or grant initiatives, many adult learner programs have often been fully engaged in both qualitative and quantitative assessment efforts to both justify and substantiate their programs—and even their existence.

Now, however, defining best practices has become more important than ever, given how ubiquitous adult programs are among for-profit and nonprofit institutions. When faced with the incredible range of options, how is an adult learner able to choose which programs are best? Or, when an institution seeks to either begin or improve its adult learner program, how can that program identify those practices that constitute an ideal model? Recently, some accrediting bodies and adult learner organizations have begun to provide guidelines, criteria, and benchmarks to help respond to these questions. The results of their efforts are provided in this chapter along with a profile of what might serve as the epitome of a lifelong learning program at the college level.

Guidelines and Principles

As noted in previous chapters, more institutions of higher education are offering courses, certificates, and degrees to adult learners in the 21st century than ever before. At a time when the adult learner is pervasive, the number of schools that exclusively serve the traditional student population continues to shrink. Adult learning programs are closer than ever to substantiating some predictions and concerns that have been envisioned and expressed within three notable commissions created to examine this topic during the past 30 years. These include the Commission on Non-Traditional Study with its important report, *Diversity by Design,* published in 1973; the Commission on Higher Education and the Adult Learner, which published its report, *Adult Learners: Key to the Nation's Future,* in 1984; and the Commission for a Nation of Lifelong Learners that assembled a stellar group to meet for two years before publishing *A Nation Learning: Vision for the 21st Century,* in 1997. These three commissions have provided the foundation for much of the work and dialogue that have defined the development of adult learner programs that have taken place within the academy in recent years. As colleges and universities seek to respond to the growing adult market, the role the adult learner will play in their mission is likely to become more central in their consciousness. That is, the institution will need to make a systemic commitment to this population so that their assimilation and experience can be meaningful. In order to survive what has become a significantly more competitive (sometimes even cutthroat) environment, institutions of higher education must become more sensitive to market pressures than ever before or risk losing their competitive edge. However, this market pressure can also stimulate practices that dilute or undermine the integrity of the institution. In many cases, schools that respond to market pressures may concentrate almost exclusively on the significant income potential that adult learners often represent without giving consideration to the special issues that relate to these students. The Task Force on Adult Degree Completion Programs (2000) concluded that when institutional support is not forthcoming, the following weaknesses may emerge:

1) Adult degree completion programs are operated as appendages if they are not integrated into the whole of the institution.

2) Adult degree completion programs are unlikely to be outcomes based.

3) Insufficient professional development activities are made available for faculty and staff.

4) Adult degree completion programs that are not integrated into the institution's culture receive little attention in areas such as governance, budgeting and planning, faculty involvement, peer recognition, and the sharing of resources. (p. 6)

The concerns expressed here reflect the issues that are more likely to arise when dynamic changes take place on the campus. With increased adult enrollment, colleges and universities across the nation have entered into an often-animated dialogue concerning identity and mission, with special attention focused on integrating meaningful lifelong learning into the fabric of the institution. Indeed, the role and function of continuing education has been called upon to service new populations of adult learners at every point along the learning continuum. As a result, some schools have applied extra effort to ensure that the term "lifelong learning" is not merely empty rhetoric. But without guidelines and models, this dialogue has often faced special challenges as schools seek the frequently daunting task of trying to reconcile, in some meaningful way, their adult programs with their institutional mission and purpose. To alleviate this situation, at least three organizations have identified what they believe constitutes good practice for adult learners by outlining specific guidelines or expectations. Each organization serves an appropriate and somewhat specialized constituency.

The American Council on Education

The American Council on Education (ACE), in partnership with the Adult Higher Education Alliance, published *Principles of Good Practice for Alternative and External Degree Programs for Adults* in 1990. This document still serves as a baseline for any discussion concerning this topic:

1) **Mission Statement:** The program has a mission statement that reflects an educational philosophy, goals, purposes, and general intent and clearly complements the institutional mission.

2) **Personnel—Faculty and Academic Professionals:** Faculty and academic professional working in alternative and external degree programs share a commitment to serve adult learners and have the attitudes,

knowledge, and skills required to reach, advise, counsel, and assist such students.

3) **Learning Outcomes:** Clearly articulated programmatic learning outcomes frame the comprehensive curriculum as well as specific learning experiences; in developing these outcomes, the program incorporates general student goals.

4) **Learning Experiences:** The program is designed to provide diverse learning experiences that respond to the characteristics and contexts of adult learners while meeting established academic standards.

5) **Assessment of Student Learning:** The assessment of a student's learning is used to determine the achievement of comprehensive and specific learning outcomes.

6) **Student Services:** The policies, procedures, and practices of the program take into account the conditions and circumstances of adult learners and promote the success of those students.

7) **Program Administration:** The administrative structures and the human, fiscal, and learning resources are sufficient, appropriate, and stable for accomplishing the program mission.

8) **Program Evaluation:** Evaluation of the program involves faculty, academic professionals, administrators, and students on a continuing, systematic basis to assure quality and standards, and to stimulate program improvement. (pp. 8–9)

The Council for Adult and Experiential Learning

The Council for Adult and Experiential Learning's (CAEL) publication, *Principles of Effectiveness for Serving Adult Learners in Higher Education* (2000a), is part of a long-term project that traces its roots back to a combined publication between CAEL and ACE in 1993: *Adult Degree Programs: Quality Issues, Problem Areas, and Actions Steps.* Among their conclusions:

> One of the major outcomes of the research, information gathering, and sharing and planning activities involved in the preparation of this paper is the conclusion of the CAEL/ACE steering committee that the identification and

> targeting of abuse is not likely to be the most effective strategy for addressing problems of quality in adult programs. Rather, a strategy that builds consumer awareness of quality issues, promotes models of excellence, and fosters a climate of continuous improvement is more likely to succeed in producing a climate within which abuses are less likely to flourish. (p. 27)

Following that first step, CAEL has been carefully systematic in its design of this project to identify ways higher education can better serve adult learners and their employers. CAEL then introduced a benchmarking study that is covered in more detail later in this chapter. The study was designed to find and examine best practices at colleges and universities. These findings, published in *Best Practices in Adult Learning* (Flint & Associates, 1999), served as a foundation for further exploration on this topic where CAEL continued to seek and identify best practices at Adult Learning Focused Institutions (ALFI). This dimension of the CAEL project is also detailed later in this chapter. Finally, another step was to publish the *Principles of Effectiveness for Serving Adult Learners in Higher Education* (2000a) (the principles are listed under "Reference Points" later in this chapter).

Higher Learning Commission of the North Central Association

The Board of Trustees of the Higher Learning Commission of the North Central Association (NCA) commissioned a Task Force on Adult Degree Completion Programs in 2000. Since an accrediting body's perspective and constituents are dissimilar from the two previous citations that encompass adult learning organizations, these principles may tend to be a bit more global. In this application, however, the institutional guidelines and recommendations may also serve to provide meaningful criteria for the unit devoted to administering the adult learner.

Mission

- The adult degree completion programs are consistent with and integral to the institution's mission.

Resources

- Faculty members share a commitment to serve adult learners, bring appropriate credentials to the work assignments, and participate in determining policies that govern adult degree completion programs.
- Full-time and part-time faculty members who work in adult degree completion programs participate in professional development activities that focus on the needs of adult learners.
- The institution provides an adequate organizational structure, administrative support, and financial resources to ensure the effectiveness of adult degree completion programs.
- Adequate institutional resources are committed to the adult degree completion programs to ensure quality and appropriate student services.
- The institution provides timely and adequate access to the range of student services—including admissions, financial aid, academic advising, delivery of course materials, and counseling and placement services—needed to ensure academic success.
- The institution ensures access to learning resources, technology, and facilities to support its adult degree completion programs.

Educational Programs and Other Services

- The adult degree completion programs that the institution offers are in subject areas that are consistent with the institution's mission.
- The adult degree completion programs have clearly stated requirements and outcomes in the areas of the major and general education.
- Adult degree completion programs and courses that are offered in distance delivery modalities conform to the *Guidelines for Distance Education* cited in the NCA *Handbook for Accreditation.*
- The assessment of student learning outcomes is a standard practice in all adult degree completion programs and is linked to program improvement.
- The institution uses a variety of acceptable methodologies (e.g., examinations in subject areas; assessment of prior learning using principles

advocated by organizations such as the Council for Adult and Experiential Learning (CAEL), the American Council on Education (ACE), the Adult Higher Education Alliance, and the Middle States Commission on Higher Education (MSA/CHE); and its faculty is trained in how to use and apply these methods.

- Multiple measures (portfolio assessment, capstone courses, oral examinations, juried examinations, standardized national exams, locally developed tests, performance on licensure, and certification/professional exams) are used to assess the learning outcomes of students enrolled in adult degree completion programs.
- Adult degree completion programs address students' education and career goals at the time of reentry and throughout the degree completion process in order to assess the learning they will need and to help them reach their goals.

Planning

- Consideration of adult degree completion programs is integrated into the institution's planning and evaluation processes in order to ensure continuous improvement in the offerings.

Integrity

- The institution has processes in place to ensure that the adult degree completion programs it sponsors are offered with integrity and are responsive to learners and the community.
- The institution that partners with another organization to deliver an adult degree completion program is knowledgeable of the "Good Practices in Contractual Arrangements Involving Courses and Programs" published by the NCA Commission on Institutions of Higher Education and uses the document as a guide in ensuring the integrity of its program. (pp. 6–7)

An Additional Point of View

Lifelong Learning at Its Best (Maehl, 2000), based on a national study funded by the Kellogg Foundation, presents one other perspective regarding this issue. The author examines over 30 of the most successful adult learning programs in the country and summarizes those characteristics that stand out in his experience of seeking and identifying the "best of the best" among adult programs:

- Clarity of mission and purpose
- A strong commitment, including funding, to undertake the program
- Appropriate match between learners and the program, as exhibited through recruitment, admission, entry, and continuing practices
- Provision of a favorable climate of learning, including advising and other services
- Adaptability to learner circumstances, either individually or in context
- Recognition and involvement of learner experience
- Commitment and development of faculty and staff
- Clearly identified administration and governance
- Ongoing program evaluation and documentation
- Positive program impact and future prospects (p. 268)

In his conclusion, Maehl cites explicit examples for each of the criteria indicated above. He also notes, "The programs described in this book participate in all these characteristics, although to varying degrees. In summarizing them here, I highlight some of the more prominent examples of each" (p. 268).

Benchmarks and Models

Although two books have been devoted to the topic of identifying best practices and benchmarks among adult programs, *Lifelong Learning at Its Best* (Maehl, 2000) and *Best Practices in Adult Learning* (Flint & Associates, 1999), there is substantial evidence that this is only the beginning stage of what is likely to evolve in the future for adult learning programs.

Lifelong Learning at Its Best, by William H. Maehl (2000), is based on a national study and features over 30 models or cases of programs that work in terms of the goals and objectives they set themselves and the needs of the learners they serve. The author states:

> These cases are by no means exhaustive. Many other excellent programs could stand alongside them as examples. Nor should the practices described here be considered prescriptive. The purpose of these models is to be illustrative and heuristic and in the process to provide resources that can be applied in a spirit of creativity. (p. 46)

Schools identified as models include a diverse and comprehensive group of institutions that represent every regional and learning perspective: from small to large, associate to doctorate degrees, from coast to coast, and from on-site to distance delivery of learning.

Best Practices in Adult Learning, a CAEL/APQC (American Productivity & Quality Center) publication by Flint & Associates (1999), was designed as a benchmarking study to "plan, screen, review, visit sites, and report findings, as an intermediate step toward ultimately fulfilling CAEL's ALFI project. CAEL made it a point to define 'best-practice' within the focus of the study and not 'best institution for any learner'" (p. 16). Furthermore, the study had constraints that limited the number of institutions that participated. Therefore, these schools serve as prototypes rather than exemplars. As such, CAEL and the reader are able to determine a significant number of lessons learned from this study—results that may be critical when any institution seeks to determine its own set of quality indicators. The institutions that participated in this study include:

- Athabasca University, Athabasca, Alberta, Canada
- College of New Rochelle, School of New Resources, New Rochelle, New York
- DePaul University, School for New Learning, Chicago, Illinois
- Empire State College, State University of New York, Saratoga Springs, New York
- Marylhurst University, Marylhurst, Oregon
- Sinclair Community College, Dayton, Ohio

CAEL articulated its findings from the information and evidence it gathered among these six schools in *Serving Adult Learners in Higher Education* (2000b). This report served to further the discussion among CAEL constituents, resulting in the ALFI principles of effectiveness.

Just as colleges and universities have long sought to achieve high rankings in the various publications that classify schools for potential students, adult programs are just now beginning to be singled out for their excellence. Furthermore, one of the lessons learned in the jazz education movement (see Chapter 1) has been that there is a certain prestige associated with schools and programs that have achieved a superior level of success. Therefore, it is clear that benchmarking, identifying model programs, and ranking them will continue to grow for adult learning programs as the century progresses.

Reference Points: Best Practices Identified

As CAEL is at the forefront of this movement at this time, it is appropriate to examine what credentials CAEL believes must reside in a program to qualify it as an ALFI program. *The Principles of Effectiveness for Serving Adult Learners in Higher Education* (2000a) are designed as a framework for assessing institutional practice and determining how to better meet the needs of adults and their employers. In addition to the principles, CAEL has also provided a number of explanatory remarks that provide additional comments and provide greater breadth for each principle.

Outreach: The institution conducts its outreach to adult learners by overcoming barriers in time, place, and tradition in order to create lifelong access to educational opportunities.

Life and career planning: The institution addresses adult learners' life and career goals before or at the onset of enrollment in order to assess and align its capacities to help learners reach their goals.

Financing: The institution promotes choice using an array of payment options for adult learners in order to expand equity and financial flexibility.

Assessment of learning outcomes: The institution defines and assesses the knowledge, skills, and competencies acquired by adult learners both from the curriculum and from life/work experience in order to assign credit and confer degrees with rigor.

Teaching-learning process: The institution's faculty uses multiple methods of instruction (including experiential and problem-based methods) for adult learners in order to connect curricular concepts to useful knowledge and skills.

Student support systems: The institution assists adult learners using comprehensive academic and student support systems in order to enhance students' capacities to become self-directed, lifelong learners.

Technology: The institution uses information technology to provide relevant and timely information and to enhance the learning experience.

Strategic partnerships: The institution engages in strategic relationships, partnerships, and collaborations with employers and other organizations in order to develop and improve educational opportunities for adult learners. (pp. 11–15)

●●●●●

This case study attempts to synthesize the various principles and guidelines contained in this chapter into an idealized model for an institution of higher learning. Since it is impossible to convey in a single model the incredible array of institutions that are available to learners today, this case study seeks to use, as its foundation, a rather conventional private four-year college that introduced adult learning programs in the early 1980s. As an added dimension, given the guidelines and principles from this chapter, readers are strongly encouraged to create their own "University of Topia" since this is the perfect opportunity to assemble all the information offered in the first section of this book into a single effort that is designed to capture "analysis, synthesis, and evaluation"— i.e., the higher levels of Bloom's taxonomy. Using your institution as a starting point, you may wish to build your own hypothetical adult program, college, or university at this time (think of it as an exercise in envisioning the future).

Case Study: The University of Topia

The University of Topia is located in the Midwest, in a town only 12 miles from its state's largest city. In 1947, Topia College opened its doors as a small liberal arts school, designed primarily to attract students within a 50-mile radius. In 1995, in preparation for its 50th anniversary, it faced some serious challenges as it continued to struggle with its enrollment base of 1,350 undergraduate students. Even though faculty and staff were extremely dedicated and worked tirelessly to maintain the quality of the institution, many of the members of the college community quietly wondered whether the school could survive in the midst of growing and more aggressive competition from other schools in the area. As part of a self-reflective community dialogue, the school redefined its target population and mission, then changed its status (from college to university) in 1997—both as a result of the dialogue and the new student population it now serves.

After much discussion and analysis, faculty members recognized that almost 90% of the students enrolled at Topia were in preprofessional degree tracks (i.e., business, education, media communication, and the arts); that these disciplines represented the greatest strengths of their curriculum; and that these majors would resonate especially well with adult learners—today, a growing portion of the University of Topia (UT) student body.

Initially, faculty members were primarily anxious to retain Topia's liberal arts roots by sustaining a rather extensive core curriculum. But President C. Moore—a highly persuasive leader who had led the school for seven years to a position that was widely agreed as being "a notch above" where the institution was when he arrived—envisioned this moment as a special opportunity. Despite the progress made since Dr. Moore's arrival, the enrollment figures still inhibited meaningful expansion and fiscal opportunities. But now he was able to convince faculty members that unifying the school's mission, identity, and vision was the best way to accomplish two extremely important outcomes they all sought.

Dr. Moore suggested that his strategy—a simple redefinition of the institution that more precisely captured the school's identity—not only provided an increased potential for enrollment but also achieved a stronger sense of unity among the faculty, staff, and student body. One of the possible changes he identified as a result of this strategy was the expansion of the school's target population to include adult learners.

By the time the school actually celebrated its 50th anniversary, it had already begun to make important strides toward accomplishing its objectives. In fact, UT was beginning to accomplish something President Moore had been articulating since 1995—attract national attention for some of its "innovations." Eventually, the entire school was able to articulate its objective in a compact statement: "To become in fact and by reputation one of the nation's leaders in assessment and lifelong learning." What, specifically, did this school do that was so remarkable and impressive that by 2002, other schools often routinely sent teams to observe UT in its general operation?

Lifelong Learning I

In 1994, the academic vice president assembled a task force to assess the vitality of the continuing education program at Topia. So far, the program had served as a modest noncredit appendage to the institution since 1987, but it seemed to lack focus or definition without much growth or development during the ensuing years. Frankly, it hadn't been a very high priority until the new academic VP, Cecilia Eden, said she wanted to determine whether it might be an asset, had any potential at all, or should perhaps be eliminated. (Based upon a highly successful adult program at her previous school, she believed a comparable program would flourish at UT as well but she wanted to confirm her expectations while making certain the faculty would feel invested.) Thanks in part to a substantial grant she secured from a major corporation, task force members were able to obtain release time and expenses so that they could meet weekly, discuss salient issues, and visit various sites of model programs. The team was ready with their preliminary report after six months. They had visited four schools and read extensively about guidelines, principles, and best practices. They had interviewed representatives from the American Council on Education, the Association for Continuing Higher Education, and the Council for Adult and Experiential Learning. They also continued to use these organizations as sources as they further explored various questions and concerns. Their discussion had primarily focused on market potential for adult learners (specifically, which majors currently offered at Topia matched career needs in the area), Topia's ability to respond to the special needs of the adult learner, and how well Topia's infrastructure could serve this population. However, they also encountered some models that extended beyond the mere delivery of adult learner credit courses for certificates and degree completion that they believed would offer a particularly good fit for both the school and the community at large it served. The task force made three recommendations to the president's council:

1) Adult professional degree completion programs and certificate programs, based on the best practice guidelines they had discovered, should serve as the heart of a new proposed program called "Lifelong Learning."

2) This program should address the learning needs of all citizens in their geographic region, with the broadest possible range of options

and services available to learners, so that Topia would act as a primary learning resource center.

3) The program should seamlessly become a part of Topia's identity and mission, with full buy-in and support of all constituents within the institution.

By the time the team had its report ready, their discussions with Vice President Eden had convinced them that Topia was facing a very special opportunity. Furthermore, everyone on the task force believed that this initiative could bring the institution to an exciting new level without ever compromising its original mission. They added their third recommendation because they had encountered institutions that reflected various degrees of disconnection between the faculty members and the unit devoted to adult degree completion. Therefore, in their minds, they believed it would be essential to seek dialogues and buy-in from all faculty in order to avoid problems later. To these recommendations, President Moore, who also saw the potential this initiative represented, offered two additional provisions of his own:

1) That the school would make an ongoing commitment to first-rate faculty development activities with an expectation of mandatory participation among all stakeholders—part-time and full-time faculty and administrators. (In order to achieve this fiscally, he proposed a small "surcharge" that would be taken from every Lifelong Learning–associated tuition fee to be put into a special faculty development fund.) This strategy ensured that all Lifelong Learning instructors—often requiring special sensitivity to adult learners, new classroom formats, and other newer technologies—would reflect the most current and appropriate practices and remain state-of-the-art in their classrooms.

2) In return, capitalizing on the long series of changes he knew these initiatives would almost certainly entail, and wanting to use this opportunity to achieve a level of excellence that he had always believed the school was capable, he sought a campus-wide, concentrated effort to fully utilize program evaluation or assessment in all possible applications. In this manner, he believed the institution would achieve a twofold gain: By fully assessing any new initiative associated with Lifelong Learning, Topia would be able to create the

strongest and best possible program—especially for adult learners. And by applying these same procedures in active and meaningful ways throughout the school's everyday activities, Topia could become a showcase model for other institutions.

While he believed that creating an entirely new initiative like Lifelong Learning provided the perfect incentive to utilize program evaluation in order to determine its justification, he also recognized that it was more likely to be meaningful if it was designed to be endemic rather than merely restricted to one program. (Dr. Eden had been instrumental in his thinking when, shortly after she was hired, she pointed out that Topia would be undergoing its next accreditation visit in six years and they still needed to fully implement a strong assessment plan anyway.) In turn, he was convinced that even though Topia was not a particularly large or well-known institution, it had the means to accomplish both of these outcomes and, by doing so, it could gain a national reputation. This was President Moore's vision, articulated frequently from the moment the task force first made its report to the assembled campus community one month after its initial report to the president's council.

Program Assessment

One of the concepts the task force encountered that helped to formulate President Moore's position in the first place was the paucity of program evaluation and program documentation that was repeatedly noted in the literature it encountered. Explicitly, it cited a quote from Maehl (2000):

> Most programs express a desire to undertake such follow-up study or have plans to do so. Yet many programs are small and have limited staff and find additional evaluation tasks difficult to carry out. *It would be useful to undertake a comprehensive study of adult program evaluation and to offer support to those programs with meager evaluation resources.* (p. 279)

(In fact, President Moore later confirmed that: "When I read those lines, it was like the final pieces of a puzzle fit together in my brain! I knew program assessment was something that was inherently good for the institution. At the same time, I realized that this was an initiative that could provide us with a significant reputation.) Because of the clarity of his vision and his ability to articulate it in a manner that reinforced the benefits to all stakeholders, faculty members were strongly supportive of the dual concepts of creating a new unit in Lifelong Learning and making a meaningful commitment to program assessment.

Two new task forces (assessment and Lifelong Learning) were quickly created and, once again, the school was able to obtain a generous grant, this time from a charitable trust. The grant allowed the Topia faculty and administration to move forward quickly and interactively by means of various groups that worked throughout the summers on the numerous problems they faced. It also provided faculty members with the opportunity to actively learn about the best practices associated with each of these issues through visitations—either to the model sites or conferences—so long as the faculty member would then report back to his or her colleagues. As a result of all the campus dialogue and interaction, Topia achieved one of President Moore's main agendas within the first year after the report was initially made. Because the task forces required a level of focus, investment, interaction, and energy that the campus had never experienced before, he now saw the entire campus community as unified. Indeed, these would continue to be the traits that were most often cited over the next few years as various schools sent individuals or teams to observe UT's model programs in assessment and Lifelong Learning.

The program assessment was designed to be ubiquitous. Every class, course, minor, major, certificate, or degree was built with specific, measurable outcomes that continued to be monitored and adjusted. The entire system required a great deal of faculty interaction with all faculty members empowered and invested in the institution's health and well-being. At the end of 2002, when President Moore retired, the University of Topia remained small, but its impact was significant. Not only was there a growing body of feature articles and conference presentations about the school, but many schools now model their own assessment programs and/or Lifelong Learning programs on the UT concept.

Lifelong Learning II

The first credit segments of the new Center for Lifelong Learning (CLL) at UT were offered in the fall of 1996. After much careful discussion and analyses of both the needs of the community and the capacity of the school to deliver new formats (especially entailing accelerated courses), the CLL first offered a certificate in human resources. For many of the primary stakeholders, a certificate was a perfect way to begin since it only entailed six courses, the entire certificate could be completed in two semesters, and through careful assessment, the CLL could monitor every aspect of their program in order to determine how and what they could improve. One further advantage UT gained from this experience was that it responded to the adult learners' sense of urgency with a quick resolution of their studies.

By completing one semester-long course bundled with two eight-week accelerated courses, students were offered the opportunity to complete the entire certificate quickly, but without having to take more than two courses at any one time. Based on surveys, the CLL determined that the majority of adult learners interested in the program in their area preferred weekend courses. Therefore, the semester-long course met for 150 minutes each Saturday morning, followed by a 15-minute break, and then an eight-week "QuikCourse" that met for three hours. In this manner, students only needed to come to campus once per week. As an added feature, UT was able to offer a Saturday nursery school for those students who needed its services.

But concurrently, the program also wanted to address other constituents. Once again, responding to community needs, CLL helped create a Senior Institute for Learners (SIL) that offered noncredit courses for members of the community 60 or older. Within two years, the program has become self-sustaining, and not only is there no cost to UT, it contributes a healthy portion of its income back to the institution. At the same time, in an effort to provide instruction for younger members in the community, the Departments of Art and Music began offering courses and lessons (with some programs even specially designed for toddlers), while the Department of Communications created a series of workshops on journalism. In fact, Debbie Koffee, the newly appointed director of CLL, often spoke about her vision of three generations of a family piling into their car on Saturday morning to come to UT to study: The youngsters to study the arts, computers, or communication, Mom to complete her certificate (or later, her degree), and Grandma and Grandpa to learn about a variety of topics in the SIL courses.

Today, all those options, and many more, are available to young and older members of the community. The CLL is also offering degrees in five majors that have a strong preprofessional orientation. They have done extensive assessment of their accelerated courses that have resulted in procedures that are now being utilized in other schools. By constantly evaluating every aspect of their program, it has been described as "organic" since it is constantly evolving and growing. But it is the byproduct of the CLL program that probably pleases Debbie Koffee the most: "As a result of the enthusiasm and support we get from our SIL program, and because of our ability to not only identify but nurture talented younger students, we have seen the UT day enrollment grow. In the case of the SIL students, their influence on their grandchildren has been remarkable and with the younger students, they already have a sense of belonging so coming here just seems natural."

As for the adult degree completion programs, the total number of students enrolled in these majors just topped the traditional day student enrollment. Projections suggest this trend is likely to continue in the future.

Conclusion

The UT story is not far-fetched. Indeed, there are many remarkable anecdotes about notable colleges and universities that create the sort of transformation and clear sense of purpose described in this study. As there are so many paths that can be taken to achieve excellence in continuing education or lifelong learning that this story is not intended to be prescriptive in any way, just illustrative of one of those paths. However, the following factors are critical: 1) good communication, 2) a unified sense of purpose, 3) a commitment to excellence, 4) a willingness to change, 5) strong assessment procedures to determine what is and what isn't working well, and 6) the capacity for everyone to be flexible and creative in their thinking.

● ● ● ● ●

Conclusion

On many campuses, a natural tension is apt to exist between the adult degree completion unit and some members of the faculty—especially those who do not work with adult learners. This seems particularly true when faculty members have any reason to assume that the unit is either attempting to dilute or diminish the quality of the school's product: its courses and degrees. These suspicions from the faculty are justified at times since there have been some instances where adult programs have not always been bound or committed to practices of excellence or high standards. Furthermore, many aspects of the adult learner are different from the traditional student—the population most familiar to the majority of faculty members. Because of these differences, there is ample opportunity to be suspicious about whether the practices most commonly associated with adult degree completion—such as prior learning assessment, accelerated courses, different admission standards, etc.—might be undermining the integrity of the institution. This is why it is so crucial to identify best practices and guiding principles for adult programs. There are a number of ways that a school can accomplish this, but they almost always start with good communication between faculty, leaders, and members of the adult program. By establishing high standards and identifying best practices, the adult program will assist the members of the faculty to see how their program can match or even exceed the standards of the institution.

At the same time, firsthand experiences may be the best way to demonstrate this. For instance, I know of a school that wanted to create a new adult learner program but the faculty members were highly skeptical and therefore reluctant to become invested. Based on his previous experience, the president of the school had seen what a good adult program could do and really wanted this program to achieve some of the same benefits. Consequently, he created an ad hoc committee of faculty leaders and asked them to candidly discuss their reservations and concerns. In part, he was able to obtain their full input when he promised them final say in whether the adult program would become a reality. At the same time, he indicated that if the school was going to add an adult program, it would demand a high degree of faculty involvement. Once they agreed to these terms, the president arranged a two-day intensive visit to one of the more successful adult programs so that the faculty leaders could determine the validity of such a program based on their best practices—standards that the new program sought to emulate. By the time the faculty members returned from their evaluative visit, they were more optimistic about their own new adult program. Ultimately, most of these faculty leaders became the primary members of the adult learning advisory committee. Today, that program has become one of the jewels in the school's crown.

When done well, adult programs quickly become issues of passion. I continue to encounter faculty members and administrators who get very excited as soon as they begin talking about their adult learners. "Love" is the word they tend to use when they describe how they feel about their students. Many are quick to tell stories about how much more engaged and excited they are about teaching because of their experiences with adult learners. This is not to suggest that teaching adult learners is for everyone (it's not—it's really about good fit), but give me a program where I can work with individuals who feel passionately about their field and I'll show you a program that can achieve very special heights.

REFERENCES

American Council on Education & the Adult Higher Education Alliance. (1990). *Principles of good practice for alternative and external degree programs for adults.* Washington, DC: American Council on Education.

Commission for a Nation of Lifelong Learners. (1997). *A nation learning: Vision for the 21st century.* Albany, NY: Regents College.

Commission on Higher Education and the Adult Learner. (1984). *Adult learners: Key to the nation's future.* Washington, DC: Author.

Commission on Non-Traditional Study. (1973). *Diversity by design.* San Francisco, CA: Jossey-Bass.

Council for Adult and Experiential Learning & the American Council on Education. (1993, March). *Adult degree programs: Quality issues, problem areas, and action steps.* Chicago, IL: Author.

Council for Adult and Experiential Learning. (2000a). *Principles of effectiveness for serving adult learners in higher education.* Chicago, IL: Author.

Council for Adult and Experiential Learning. (2000b). *Serving adult learners in higher education.* Chicago, IL: Author.

Flint, T. A., & Associates. (1999). *Best practices in adult learning: A CAEL/APQC benchmarking study.* New York, NY: Forbes Custom Publishing.

Maehl, W. H. (2000). *Lifelong learning at its best: Innovative practices in adult credit programs.* San Francisco, CA: Jossey-Bass.

Task Force on Adult Degree Completion Programs. (2000, June). *Adult degree completion programs.* Retrieved June 5, 2001, from http://www.ncacihe.org/resources/adctf/ADCPRept.pdf

Part Two

Where Adult Learners Begin Their Educational Journey

5

Why Adult Learners Seek College-Level Learning

Overview

When a college or university accepts a new adult learner, the student's history and background are critical factors regarding how that individual is likely to view his or her existence on campus. Furthermore, their sense of purpose—why they even seek learning at the college level in the first place—is different from their younger classmates. Consequently, professors and administrators are wise to consider these issues when they interact with their adult students. This is all the more true when one recognizes how important these issues are to the adult learner.

Typically, there are two competing, though not mutually exclusive, reasons that motivate adult learners to either return or seek admission to higher education. Each of these issues will be examined in detail under the descriptive captions "The Wakeup Call" and "Now It's My Turn." In addition, two case studies are included in this chapter to illustrate how adult students arrive at that point where they are prepared to transform their lives as a result of the simple action of enrolling in college.

Background

When an adult seeks admission to a college or university, his or her story is usually much more dramatic and emotionally laden than is the case for the typical 18-year-old. Understanding the motivation for these students is extremely useful and should be taken into consideration when interacting with these students in any regard. It is also important to understand just who these students are and how their background colors what they bring to the classroom. As adult learners proceed through their collegiate studies, many tend to carry their academic past with them. Indeed, most adult learners are all too aware of their own perceived weaknesses and deficiencies (sometimes real, but just as often imagined). This situation also confirms another problem that many adult learners experience: issues of self-esteem.

In contrast to the traditional student's path—typically laid out in a neat, four-year, nonstop, linear grid—the route adult learners are apt to take to complete their degree is more likely to resemble a maze. While 18- to 22-year-olds normally follow a tidy, regimented trail toward graduation, the pathway for adult students often reflects obstacles, bumps, and junctions—a full spectrum of situations that includes starts and restarts (sometimes featuring extended breaks in between), delayed enrollment, attendance at multiple schools, and other options that challenge the very perseverance of the adult learner. To compound the issue, adult learners almost always express a sense of urgency regarding their need to complete their schooling as quickly as possible. These conflicting aspects of the adult learner often confound administrators, since it is more of a challenge to anticipate scheduling needs or to monitor enrollments from one term to the next when students don't fit into neat little units. In short, adult student enrollment behavior tends to be volatile—subject not only to external factors like the economy or workplace pressures (such as travel assignments, special projects, reduction of tuition assistance, etc.), but also to many internal situations such as family crises or health-related problems. In the latter instance, the problem may reside with the student or with any one of as many as three generations that the adult learner often serves in a caretaker role.

Even though adult learners are highly motivated, going to school is not always their top priority, especially when the needs of their loved ones are concerned. On the other hand, completing a degree or certificate is typically high on their long-range list of objectives, making perseverance one of the primary virtues attributed to adult learners. This pattern may frustrate administrators or faculty who don't fully conceptualize adult learners as a phenomenon but merely see them as a statistic or want them to function in the predictable manner of most traditional students. But adult learners are usually so burdened that they often have little margin for any additional complication in their already busy lives. Something as simple as the illness of a child can seriously jeopardize their ability to successfully sustain a class or enroll for the next term. As a result, adults tend to pose a greater challenge for both faculty and the institution's infrastructure. Indeed, this is one reason why many benchmark programs for adult learners try to provide a wide array of choices when it comes to course formats, schedules, meeting dates, times, and durations when compared with the more straightforward, inside the box options normally associated with day programs. To the extent possible, the greater flexibility regarding scheduling options for adult learners often brings healthier retention and enrollments. (Conversely, this can be one of the greater inherent challenges associated with cohort programs with their often rigid format and schedule.) It is also why meaningful advising is so frequently cited as essential for quality adult learning programs.

Programs that respond with flexible options for their adult learners often hold greater appeal among this population. Consequently, an unwillingness to work with or be sensitive to the special needs of adult learners are surefire ingredients for operating a potentially defective adult learning program.

When adult learners first hear the story of legendary baseball manager Leo Durocher's (perhaps known best for coining the phrase, "Nice guys finish last") famous encounter with an umpire, many find they can relate to it. Durocher was known for his temper and spirited displays when he disagreed with umpires. It was during one such dispute that Durocher found himself shouting at the umpire after one of his players was called out, and to demonstrate how upset he was, he kicked the umpire in the shins. Well, the umpire kicked Durocher right back. This action infuriated Leo even more so that he felt provoked to kick the umpire once again. The umpire, in turn, kicked him in the shins one more time. As Durocher told the story, it was only as he was kicking the umpire for the third time that the thought finally entered his consciousness that the umpire was wearing shin guards, so Durocher's kicks were not really doing much damage. Furthermore, he also concluded that the rather painful damage he was suffering in return could end only if he changed his own behavior. For many adult learners, it sometimes takes the combination of pain (or at least, the threat of pain) and special insights to provide the inspiration and motivation for seeking college-level learning. Like Durocher, many adult learners only see the benefits of changing their behavior when they feel forced to take action or to reduce their own "pain."

Flashpoints in the Workplace

Impulse

For adult learners, the workplace is most frequently cited as the locus where educational change is likely to begin. A college degree has become a necessity for success in our knowledge-based society. According to the National Center for Education Statistics (1998), 13.7% of the population 25 years or older had less than five years of elementary school in 1940. At that time in our nation's history, the conventional baseline prerequisite for many jobs (even those above the minimum wage standard) did not necessarily require a high school diploma.

Today, the standards have dramatically changed. More than 90% of the 25 or older population have at least completed high school. A significant and growing number of job requirements have set the minimum baseline standard at a college undergraduate degree. Indeed, persons today who only possess a high school diploma are often restricted in the job market in much the same way as their ancestors were who had not acquired a diploma: They are relegated to those positions labeled "unskilled." According to the Association of American Colleges and Universities (2002), "Possession of a college degree now means substantially what a high school diploma meant a hundred years ago; it is the place where most careers begin and without it, people find themselves stuck in dead-end jobs" (p. 1).

As late as the 1960s and 1970s, it was not at all unusual to encounter references to the "self-made" executive who had achieved an elevated position despite only possessing a high school diploma—and sometimes, not even that! In the land of opportunity, it was often stated that hard work and initiative were all you needed to succeed in America. Today, on the other hand, while a handful of exceptions may still exist, every kind of occupation has seen a dramatic increase in education requirements, and jobs that employ the most skilled workers are growing the fastest (Carnevale, 2000).

In 2001, Aslanian confirmed previous research studies when she revealed that job advancement is an extremely strong motivator for adults to seriously consider college enrollment. In many cases, businesses and corporations have integrated policies into the workplace that reinforce the importance of lifelong learning. Several studies have indicated that whereas employers were once reluctant to support their employees' pursuit of additional education in the fear that if they were better educated they would consider moving elsewhere, most employers today realize they can't survive without a well-educated workforce that is committed to sustaining the company's knowledge base. Consequently, a growing number of employers have taken a more proactive stance in supporting their employees' pursuit of higher education (Draves, 1997; Maehl, 2000).

Nonetheless, many adult learners who seek a college degree have also been found to do so as a result of internal motivation. That is, their decision to enroll is most often due to their own sense of ambition rather than a job requirement. Although tuition support from employers often provides an additional incentive factor that may help tip the scales in decision-making, a more likely scenario often involves a message—sometimes blatant, sometimes implied—that workers who are not degreed are less likely (or even unlikely) to gain promotions. So while many adult students may seek to enroll in order to fulfill their own personal goals (that is, they see themselves as having something to prove to themselves or others), the primary impulse for their decision often tends to be work related.

Motivation

One of the major characteristics of adult learners—high motivation with a strong sense of purpose—can be attributed to careful deliberation before making the commitment to obtain a degree. Research suggests that an adult student's motivation may be the best predictor for academic achievement (Merriam & Caffarella, 1991). Typically, the student's motivation is a direct result of reflection and careful consideration—that is, unlike traditional students who often enter college automatically (often without a strong sense of purpose or direction), adults tend to carefully weigh their options since they are more likely to fully understand the risks. Furthermore, adult learners usually face a significant financial burden, often without benefit of the outside (e.g., parental) support traditional students are able to enjoy. Consequently, this is a decision that almost always involves significant sacrifice on the part of the adult learner, but also typically holds strong potential for the successful graduate to improve his or her career. So when an adult learner does decide to matriculate, it is likely to be with a much greater sense of purpose.

Almost all adult learners express a strong sense of urgency. Starting later than their peers is clearly a contributing factor, but research indicates that one other factor may provide an even stronger incentive to finish their studies as quickly as possible. Although adult learners may not have read the research, they quickly grasp that one of the most dynamic aspects of sustaining their studies is based on their endurance, stamina, and perseverance. Horn's (1996) study of persistence and attainment determined that compared with traditional students, nontraditional students (defined as possessing up to seven characteristics: financial independence, part-time attendance, delayed enrollment, full-time work, dependents, single parenthood, and lack of a high school diploma) are negatively related to persistence and attainment. Compared with traditional students, nontraditional students were more likely to change their degree objective or leave without a degree. In large part, this accounts for the intense level of urgency cited among many adult learners since their likelihood for completion diminishes with time.

The "Spark"

In some instances, the decision for an adult to pursue a degree is not the result of long, careful deliberation so much as an isolated, shocking moment of reality and insight. Adult admission counselors encounter numerous stories relating to this phenomenon. Typically, the person is up for a promotion, has had previous success with his or her career, and has little warning that the company they work for is unwilling to sustain the current situation. An increasing number of companies have specific policies regarding how far an employee can advance without a degree. For many adult learners, their previous successes may have provided them with a false sense of security so that they don't see any need to pursue or complete a degree.

Although many of the adult students who encounter this sort of situation may not have the luxury of reflection and introspection that some of their fellow learners experience, most are still able to fully embrace their roles as college students with enthusiasm and commitment. These students have probably encountered colleagues who found themselves in the same circumstance and either resisted degree completion or for some reason were not able to obtain a degree. Perhaps these colleagues assessed their situation and believed that their knowledge alone would sustain their position, but corporations are littered with very knowledgeable and experienced workers whose progress has been frozen and who may even have to report to younger, less-experienced bosses with more marketable credentials. If a potential student has observed this phenomenon, fear of ending up in the same condition can serve as a strong incentive.

The workplace is also the stimulus for another phenomenon: One need only spend a few minutes scanning the employment section of any major metropolitan paper to realize that the number of new careers available on the market today is rapidly expanding. Not only are there positions available but they represent career paths and job descriptions that, for the most part, didn't exist until very recently. Although technology often plays a role in the formation of these positions, this is not always the case. These jobs may also reflect a rapidly changing and more complex society rather than simply the emergence of technology. But the obverse is true as well: If there are new positions and career paths available now that didn't exist even last year, there are also some positions and career paths that are being eliminated. In either case, the result is much the same—a strong incentive from within the workplace for adults to seek further education.

The Disenchanted (Students and Faculty)

Not all adults are happy about feeling forced to pursue college-level studies and so some approach their situation with resentment. Even though they intend to receive a degree, they may do so begrudgingly and/or by following the path of least resistance. They are more likely to miss classes or be tardy, even when the classes are accelerated. The quality of their work tends to be consistently inferior since they are less likely to be invested in actually learning the material, resulting in poor grades. For this type of student, good grades are not the objective. Their interest in is "getting done," getting courses "out of the way," and receiving closure "as fast as possible." In the academy, these are the students who tend to give all adult learners poor reputations. They provide anecdotal fuel for those faculty members who are likely to speak out against adult learners in the first place. Worse still, while there are always some adult students who seem capable of fulfilling this role, there are also some faculty members who are eager to portray these students as typical of all adult learners. Perhaps both groups are a necessary evil on most campuses but neither serves the needs of adult learners very well. In part, this may be due to the stress of ongoing and accelerated change, resulting in behavior that reflects their inability to cope.

The Wakeup Call

There is a single metaphor that appears repeatedly among incoming adult students as they attempt to illustrate or articulate their situation. Although the variations are endless, the essential story or explanation goes something like this:

> I feel like I have qualified to run in a big marathon. I'm all prepared and ready to go. But the morning of the race, something happens (the power goes off, the alarm clock doesn't work right, etc.) and, much to my horror, I oversleep. I rush to throw my clothes on and take a cab to the race site. When I get there, I can see way down the street where there is this huge, dark mass of people. I can just barely make them out but I decide I want to be in the race anyway. I already know I'm not going to be able to finish first but I believe I can probably run better than some others in the race and I don't think I will end up last. In fact, even as I begin to run, I consider redefining what it means to "win" in this race. And every minute I race, it becomes clearer to me that I would prefer to have at least tried rather than just give up. And so I run with greater enthusiasm and motivation than many of my fellow runners.

It doesn't take a degree in psychology to see what this story represents to adult learners as they begin their studies. This image is reported so frequently that it clearly evokes many of the thoughts and concerns confronting adult learners as they become acclimated to the notion of pursuing a degree or certificate. Among other issues, it conveys their sense of urgency particularly well, and also describes an epiphany that many adults report experiencing as part of their reflective process during the formative stages of their studies. These events clearly bring adult learners to a new and different place in their growth. Once they gain insight from that moment—when they realize how necessary a college education is—their sense of urgency tends to kick in as well. The process is, in fact, an example of transformative learning.

In her article "Teaching for Transformation," Patricia Cranton (2002) has a brief but thoroughly comprehensive description of the theory upon which this activity is based:

> At its core, transformative learning theory is elegantly simple. Through some event, which could be as traumatic as losing a job or as ordinary as an unexpected question, an individual becomes aware of holding a limiting or distorted view. If the individual critically examines this view, opens herself to alternatives, and consequently changes the way she sees things, she has transformed some part of how she makes meaning out of the world. (p. 65)

Although Cranton focuses on the use of this theory in the classroom, the applications also function especially well to describe the phenomenon many adult learners experience as precursors to their matriculation. Cranton identifies the facets of this theory, and while not linear, most, if not all, of these facets are experienced by adults as they prepare themselves for pursuing studies at the collegiate level. The facets are comprised of the following:

- An activating event that typically exposes a discrepancy between what a person has always assumed to be true and what has just been experienced, heard, or read
- Articulating assumptions, that is, recognizing underlying assumptions that have been uncritically assimilated and are largely unconscious
- Critical self-reflection, that is, questioning and examining assumptions in terms of where they came from, the consequences of holding them, and why they are important
- Being open to alternative viewpoints
- Engaging in discourse, where evidence is weighed, arguments assessed, alternative perspectives explored, and knowledge constructed by consensus
- Revising assumptions and perspectives to make them more open and better justified
- Acting on revision, behaving, talking, and thinking in a way that is congruent with transformed assumptions or perspectives (p. 66)

For many adults seeking admission, the critical self-reflection stage may be particularly important, since this activity is often crucial in helping to define their motivation and long-range objectives—both significant factors in predicting success. Furthermore, although the wakeup call may be broadly defined by these circumstances and situations, the individual reasons for this epiphany are extremely broad and far-reaching. For instance, Fungaroli Sargent (2000) cites more than 21 scenarios of adult learners seeking either reentry to college (after having had time to develop and mature) or admission (after having any variety of interventions that otherwise inhibited that person from previously attending school). Although the stories are extremely diverse, it is the internal process—the reflection, insights, and vision that are common threads woven throughout—that mark these experiences as especially relevant to the adult learner. Indeed, these wakeup calls account for why so many adult learners end up in school even when they don't necessarily have external vocational or career motivations.

On the other hand, admission counselors who work with adult learners typically encounter two broad categories of students: those students who are returning to college, sometimes after a number of previous starts (see "Returning Students" below), and those who have no previous collegiate experience (see "Now It's My Turn" below).

Returning Students

Intermittent adult students—those who have attended college at least once in the past—often fall into two categories: those whose early experiences were marginal or unsatisfactory but who are now motivated and feel they are ready to apply themselves, and those who have been persistent, often even successful, despite multiple starts and stops (not always at the same institution). Since this second group often begins at a later point in their adult life, they are more likely to qualify for the category below. But in both cases, students tend to view their present status as "returning" to school. Furthermore, in either situation they are likely to have experienced a great deal of internalization and reflective thinking about their status and future. Because of their experiences as college students, these adult learners often see themselves as being particularly well-equipped to handle their continued schooling—that is, they are more likely to be confident of their success.

Now It's My Turn

In contrast to the intermittent adult student, the other group of adults who enter college would be considered first-time students. Women represent the majority of the students in this group, since for many decades our culture has reinforced the notion of women as primary caretakers—especially in the 21st century where the so-called sandwich generation is often called upon to see after individuals both older and younger—as well as the concept of the woman's place being in the home. Accepted value systems for the various roles of women—wife, mother, caretaker, etc.—have repeatedly encouraged them to put their life on hold while more pragmatic issues are addressed (i.e., rearing children with its attendant responsibilities, supporting a husband while he completes his degree, looking after other family members, etc.). Furthermore, a growing portion of this population is comprised of single mothers: a special challenge more likely to be facing many women as they consider pursuing a degree or certificate. But recent trends have provided many more opportunities for adults who have never attended college before, especially those women cited in the above circumstances. In many instances, these students are more likely to face additional self-doubts and lack confidence even though they may have been highly successful in other areas of their lives.

In part, this can be attributed to a disconnect between their life experiences and perceptions of what college learning entails. For various reasons, an adult learner may envision college as different from the experiences they may have had learning to be a successful PTA president, for example. Many adults considering higher education tend to have a distorted expectation of what the college requires from its students (extremely high and demanding) and what their skills and capabilities are (inadequate and woefully deficient). This disconnect tends to carry throughout much of life—where adults (especially) have romanticized the ivory tower of academe as separate, distinctive, unique, and superior to everyday life experiences.

Adults seeking admission typically find the process to be daunting and frustrating. The situation is exacerbated when institutions are insensitive to those attributes that make the adult student unique (such as having been away from high school for many years, multiple school transfer credits, outdated standardized test results, and other issues). Successful programs demystify jargon, streamline procedures, and create adult-friendly forms for the exclusive use of adult matriculants. Benchmark programs also bundle other user-friendly strategies that include sensible admission criteria and adult-dedicated admission counselors who work closely and exclusively with this population.

Whether returning to or entering higher education for the first time, all adult students tend to go through similar emotional and mental stages in preparation for school. In the majority of cases, an inner conflict, characterized by tension between the psychological reluctance to go back to school on the one hand and a compulsive desire to succeed on the other, results in highly motivated students with a clear sense of purpose and determination. Arguably, such students define many desirable attributes any faculty member is likely to seek in order to maintain a stimulating and fully engaged learning environment. Once that faculty member understands factors that may contribute to a student's reticence, he or she can create learning situations to assist the adult learner to achieve his or her full potential.

This case study embodies many typical aspects and characteristics of women students over the age of 50. Our subject, Hope, comes from a generation and culture where there were limited options or no options at all for women to pursue a college degree when she completed high school. Neither the thinking nor the support systems of those times provided the flexibility that characterizes the 21st century academy when it comes to the options and support for women students to pursue degrees or certificates. The most dynamic and gratifying elements among adult learners include the opportunities women of this generation are able to experience and enjoy today. For every woman of this generation who is now returning to college after having started at the traditional age, there are four "Hopes" who are only now beginning their college experience. It's no wonder this is a daunting task!

Case Study: Hope

Like many women of her generation, 53-year-old Hope didn't really seem to have any options when she graduated from high school in the 1960s. Indeed, she now describes her life as being predetermined: "get a job right out of high school, get married, have children, help support the family, put the children through school." For Hope, this included working as a secretary in a local school district to send her two daughters to college—the first generation in her family to enroll and graduate.

And, then, suddenly, she found herself an empty-nester with a sense of incompletion. In the midst of a conversation between Hope and her daughters—both home for the holidays from their jobs as professionals—someone mentioned that it wasn't too late for Hope to attend college. "For me," Hope explained, "it was like I had this sudden revelation in my brain, but also my heart, and I immediately knew this is what I wanted to do more than anything."

When Hope thought about it, the reason she didn't go to college in the first place had nothing to do with her intelligence or ability—it simply wasn't an option available to her at that time. She had two brothers and her father explained, when she asked, there was no way the family could afford to send all three children. He also half-jokingly explained that since she never expressed interest in either teaching or nursing, college probably wouldn't offer her any meaningful benefits anyway unless she was interested in obtaining an MRS degree.

But Hope had been a good student in high school and both her daughters reassured her that they would help in any way possible. They also emphasized that they believed in her ability to complete a college degree. Hope told her husband, "Now it's my turn. I have already helped send our daughters to college and I've made many sacrifices. I work among many folks who already possess degrees and I believe I'm every bit as capable as they are."

Fortunately, Hope's first class was a special course for adults who have never attended (or at least, not recently attended) college. In this course, Hope was provided with a number of tools and able to learn many skills designed to help her cope and survive as an adult learner. From the first class meeting, her professor, Dr. Duke, was able to emphasize that she was not alone and that the many people in her class shared her fears and concerns. But perhaps the best part was when her classmates confirmed what her professor was saying. Up to that point, it was especially hard to accept his word since her heart was pounding so loud she was certain nobody in the class could even hear the professor. But Dr. Duke continued to reassure her and provided an environment that fostered confidence and openness among the students, so that by the end of the course, Hope and her classmates felt prepared for their future classes. Perhaps even more important, however, was how confident the class felt as a result of this experience. The final project, a reflective journal, helped each student achieve a level of self-esteem—

something many of them would have been amazed to experience before the class began.

One additional feature Hope was able to appreciate as a result of this course was the level of support she had from among her loved ones. Not only did her daughters continue to reinforce their confidence in her, her husband made dinner on the nights she had classes and made certain she had a quiet space to devote to her homework. Since she discovered that some of her classmates didn't necessarily have this sort of support, she quickly learned to fully appreciate her family's love and encouragement. Not only had the course enabled Hope to understand and appreciate the support she had, it also helped her to articulate those times when she felt particularly needy.

Upon successful completion of this course, Hope began taking courses primarily from the general studies portion of the curriculum. Even though she was able to pass these courses and the introductory course had prepared her for what to expect, there were times when she questioned why she was doing this. Sometimes she would find herself in a classroom and wonder why she was there. Even worse, she often had moments of self-doubt where she couldn't believe that she would ever be able to finish. To add to the burden of her work, family, and school obligations, Hope's mother was hospitalized during this period. Ultimately, she and her husband agreed to have her mother stay at their house, at least until she was more mobile. There were many days when Hope seemed to drag from one task to the next, but her determination and perseverance never wavered. During this time she drew her strength from some of the words Dr. Duke had stated in one of her first evenings: "The highest predictor for success is the ability to persevere! Perseverance is something you need to be conscious of every day of your life." Even though this was the hardest thing she had ever done, she kept remembering those words.

There was also one other thing she had learned in Dr. Duke's course that continued to resonate in her mind. During the third class, Dr. Duke had suggested, "When you build a brick wall, concentrate on one brick at a time and the wall will take care of itself." This advice served Hope especially well when she saw some of her classmates becoming discouraged with how many years it was going to take them to complete their studies.

At long last, Hope was able to graduate. Although she was nearing retirement age, that didn't really matter to her. "For me, it has been more about the journey than seeking a new vocation," she remarked in a ceremony just preceding her graduation. "In fact," she continued, "Now that I've completed my degree, I may just decide to take some more courses."

● ● ● ● ●

This case study reflects two primary characteristics of typical adult learners. First, Amber finds herself in a working environment that almost forces her to pursue college-level studies. Then, when she discovers that she actually loves being a student, personal interventions in her life force her to "stop out" since she can't possibly sustain her studies with all the other demands being made on her. On the other hand, like so many adult learners, Amber is fiercely determined. In fact, it is this determination that often fuels the intense level of motivation that so typifies adult learners.

Case Study: Amber

Amber had come to think of herself as a late bloomer whose efforts as an adult learner have been largely defined by external forces. Despite the fact that her two sisters (one older and one younger) had both completed their degrees many years earlier, it was only two years ago that Amber felt compelled to attend college.

In large part, her decision was based on her job. She has been working as a secretary at a small company for five years. Like many mothers, Amber had begun her adult life with an entry-level position after high school. Amber worked in a small law office, doing a wide range of tasks for four years, until her first pregnancy. At the time, she and her husband agreed that her going back to work was not part of their plans. So after her first son was born, she was able to stay home and give him her full attention. Three years later, another son was born and Amber remained at home for six more years.

When she finally did return to work (to make a little money to help out), she began working at a small company. She saw herself as simply doing a job so she did not attach any special vocational meaning to it. Eventually, however, as she began to impress her bosses and coworkers with the quality of her work, she began to think more seriously about possible promotions. Finally, it was an opening that became available in the human resources area—something Amber was really interested in—which triggered a transformation in her life. When she talked with her boss about the position, he noted that she had no college-level courses or background. "Tell you what, Amber," he began, "if you promise that you will complete the Human Resources Certificate at the local college, I will see that you get this job." Since the certificate only required six courses and it could be completed in two semesters without ever taking more than two courses at any one time, she decided to discuss it with her family.

When Amber shared her interest with her husband and boys, they were supportive, though they expressed concern lest her studies interfere too much with her role as wife and mother. Everyone in the family agreed that they would use this opportunity to serve as a trial balloon since Amber's family could see that she was excited about the prospect of the new job.

Once she had completed her first class, however, Amber was very surprised about her enthusiasm for learning and described herself as "hooked." "I just can't believe how much I love being a student. Even though my days are long and the work is hard, I feel so energized by what I'm doing right now," she told the dean of the college one evening when he asked about her classes. What particularly caught his attention was how Amber's face seemed to light up with enthusiasm when discussing her studies. He had seen these signs before and felt confident that Amber would not be content to merely pursue a Certificate in Human Resources.

Amber was working harder than at any time in her life. Three courses each semester, learning a new job, plus all the tasks she had always performed at home often made her life feel like a treadmill. Though she was tired—even exhausted—she was also exhilarated by the challenges she faced and the success she was experiencing. On the other hand, her husband and boys were not always happy with the reduced amount of time Amber was able to devote to them.

The dean encountered Amber again early in her second semester. When he asked her about her studies, she replied by saying that she was seriously considering working on a degree—perhaps in business. "I'm more tired than anytime I can remember but I've also become very organized and believe I can manage to juggle my various responsibilities." The dean took note of Amber's obvious energy level, but he also observed the dark circles under her eyes and slightly disheveled appearance. It was obvious that the pace was taking a toll on Amber.

Nonetheless, the dean was shocked when he encountered Amber near the end of the semester. Nearly breaking into tears at his question of whether she had decided to pursue a degree, she replied, "I'm not going to be able to take any courses for awhile. My husband has to start working the second shift next month and there's nobody to look after my boys. To compound the issue, they are both playing soccer this fall and that means I need to attend their games on Saturdays, so I can't even take any weekend courses. I feel like there's a hole in my heart right now. As a family, we've talked about the situation. My sons said that it was so important for me to be at their soccer matches that they will forgo any weekend events for the spring semester. Likewise, my husband is trying to change his work schedule or at least be available to look after the boys during the weekend. At any rate, I *am* enrolling for courses next semester and ultimately, I *will* graduate."

Even though he was sad to see Amber suffering at the moment, there was no doubt in the dean's mind that she would ultimately succeed. Amber exuded determination, especially in the way her eyes narrowed a bit when she talked about continuing her studies.

● ● ● ● ●

CONCLUSION

Reflecting on the enormous number of challenges facing almost any adult seeking admission as a college student, it becomes easier to admire them for their strength and determination. Whereas the transition from high school directly to college is designed to be as seamless as possible, adult learners face daunting tasks in every direction—from curricular to simple problems like navigating the schedule or using the campus bookstore. The fact of the matter is that on most college campuses there are few adult-friendly aspects of the collegiate experience, as most schools are geared to service the needs of the typical 18- to 22-year-old student.

As a result, adult learners are often expected to enter a foreign (and sometimes hostile) environment and face challenges they don't necessarily feel equipped to handle given their tendencies toward lower self-esteem and lack of confidence. Nevertheless, these same adult students are likely to possess even greater levels of determination and motivation, perhaps resulting from their not feeling mainstreamed, but also because going to school for many of them represents long years of consideration and deliberation. They are especially likely to understand what's at stake with their studies and they are usually willing to take their studies more seriously as a result. In short, one of the first places to understand the notable nature of the adult learner is at their point of entry. And understanding the adult learner—especially what makes him or her different from younger classmates—will certainly assist any faculty member or administrator who works with this population.

I have worked with adult learners via accelerated evening or weekend courses for many years, and though I found their candor, level of motivation, and ability to ask searching and meaningful questions both refreshing and stimulating, at that time I don't think I ever fully appreciated the degree of sacrifice or the other challenges they continually faced. And despite the fact that I had been an adult learner myself, I never understood the phenomenon associated with my experiences—or even thought about them then in any meaningful context.

But many of the observations and conclusions I have shared throughout this book concerning the makeup and identity of adult learners and how they ultimately matriculate come from firsthand experiences and insights (particularly as a result of "transformation" courses) and extensive conversations with other practitioners in the field. Chapter 9 is devoted, in part, to the topic of transformation courses. These are courses offered at many adult learner focused institutions that are designed to perform as the adult learner equivalent to freshman introductory courses. I have found that these transformation courses (so-called because they often serve to provide a strong foundation upon which the incoming adult learner can draw to achieve success as a student) can be particularly fertile sources of insights regarding adult learners. I like to format these courses so that they are intensive "immersions," usually offered the weekend prior to the beginning of a new term. Typically, the adult learner is required to explain a bit about his or her educational journey—what led them to this point in their life—in an effort to help them see that they are not alone in their quest for college level learning.

While this insight inevitably happens, these classes always prove to be exceptionally moving and powerful. The stories the student share, the obstacles many have been forced to overcome, and the sheer determination all contribute to my sense that these students truly are courageous. And while some adult learners may also prove to be manipulative (after all, they have absorbed a great many more experiences than the typical 18- year-old) or excessively demanding (since they also have more highly refined consumer skills than their younger classmates), I can't help but admire and respect them as a group. After all, most of them are living proof that perseverance is one of the most admirable of human traits.

REFERENCES

Aslanian, C. (2001). *Adult students today.* Washington, DC: The College Board.

Association of American Colleges and Universities. (2002). *Greater expectations: A new vision for learning as a nation goes to college.* Washington, DC: Author.

Carnevale, A. P. (2000). *Help wanted... college required.* Washington, DC: Educational Testing Service.

Cranton, P. (2002, Spring). Teaching for transformation. *New Directions for Adult and Continuing Education, 93,* 63–71.

Draves, W. A. (1997). *Learning in the 21st century* (2nd ed.). Manhattan, KS: Learning Resources Network.

Fungaroli Sargent, C. (2000). *Traditional degrees for nontraditional students.* New York, NY: Farrar, Straus & Giroux.

Horn, L. (1996). *Nontraditional undergraduates, trends in enrollment from 1986–1992 and persistence and attainment among 1989–90 beginning postsecondary students* (NCES 97-578). US Department of Education, NCES. Washington, DC: US Government Printing Office.

Maehl, W. H. (2000). *Lifelong learning at its best: Innovative practices in adult credit programs.* San Francisco, CA: Jossey-Bass.

Merriam, S. B., & Caffarella, R. S. (1991). *Learning in adulthood.* San Francisco, CA: Jossey-Bass.

National Center for Education Statistics. (1989). *Projections of education statistics to 2000.* Washington, DC: National Center for Education Statistics, Office of Educational Research and Improvement, US Department of Education.

6

What Adult Learners Bring to the School

Overview

If adult learners arrive on the college campus with different reasons for pursuing degrees or certificates than their younger classmates, the differences do not simply stop at that point. As adult learners sit in the classroom absorbing new information, they tend to process what they learn in a different manner as well. Where younger students are more likely to seek theoretical perspectives in the coursework since they seldom have enough experience to apply what they have learned from that experience, adult learners almost always begin by drawing from their past experiences even when these might not apply in quite the same manner. In other words, their learning tends to take place at a higher level according to Bloom's taxonomy.

One distinctive aspect of many adult programs is their willingness to give credit for adult learners who can demonstrate that the learning they have derived from their experiences corresponds to college-level work. Good practices and guidelines for appropriate distribution of this "prior learning" credit have become a significant concern among accrediting bodies to ensure that this practice is not abused.

Thinking with Your Toes

Quantum Learning

Jane Vella (2002) points out that it was the sculptor, Rodin, who described his famous work, *The Thinker,* with the following words: "Notice how the thinker is clearly thinking with his toes" (p. 73). This evocative description not only captures the very essence of the sculpture, but, according to Vella, is the epitome of quantum learning, typically demonstrated by adult learners. She defines quantum learning as "that which uses all of the neural networks in the brain, putting things together in idiosyncratic and personal ways to make significant meaning" (p. 73). Note the constituent parts evident in this definition: 1) "putting things together," something successful adult learners seek to accomplish in order to better understand a problem or situation (that is, adult learners are more likely to think holistically); 2) "in idiosyncratic and personal ways," because adult learners process all information through their own personal frame of reference (in other words, they are more apt to draw from their own previous experiences while processing information, a typical trait of most adult learners); and 3) "to make significant meaning" is also a critical factor for adult learners since, at their foundation, they are constantly looking for relevance and validation (because, as they process information, they want affirmation that what they are learning is meaningful and useful since they are likely to consider it otherwise unnecessary). Therefore, typical adult learners are quintessential quantum learners in their behavior. For a more detailed description of how faculty can maximize quantum learning in their classroom, see Chapter 8.

Bloom's Taxonomy

In 1956, Benjamin Bloom led a group of educational psychologists to develop a classification of thinking behaviors that were perceived as important in the learning process. This became a taxonomy that included three domains: cognitive, psychomotor, and affective. Initially, this information was utilized in education (starting with early childhood) to support presentation of information and/or assessment. This taxonomy, reflecting six levels of competencies that move hierarchically from simple to complex, demonstrates different sets of skills. Although the original work was done nearly 50 years ago, it continues to enjoy widespread application today—a testimony to the reliability of the system.

Adult learners, drawing from the often-times extensive experiences life has provided them, are more likely to seek upper-level competencies as a natural extension of how they have learned to experience life and their need for relevance. Therefore, Bloom's work takes on new significance for adult learners. Each of the competencies and matching skills that are demonstrated as a result of having achieved the competencies are indicated in Figure 6.1.

FIGURE 6.1

Bloom's Taxonomy

Competence	Skills Demonstrated
Knowledge	Observe and recall information Knowledge of dates, events, places Know major ideas Mastery of basic subject matter
Comprehension	Understand information, grasp meaning Translate knowledge to a new context Interpret facts, compare, contrast, order, group, infer causes Predict consequences
Application	Use information, use methods, concepts, theories in new situations Solve problems, use required skills or knowledge
Analysis	See patterns, organize the parts, recognize hidden meanings Identify components
Synthesis	Use old ideas to create new ones Generalize from given facts Relate knowledge from several areas Predict, draw conclusions
Evaluation	Compare/discriminate between ideas Assess value of theories, make choices based on argument Verify value of evidence, recognize subjectivity

To fully understand how adult learners are often likely to absorb new information, it is helpful to review what a typical outcome derived from these same competencies might look like.

Although the taxonomy is hierarchical, it is not linear. Much like the quantum learning model described above, adult learners are most likely to spiral among and between various levels as they process new information and try to place it into a meaningful perspective. In other words, they are likely to be using the first four levels, even if the process is unconscious. Faculty members who understand that this activity is likely to be taking place as their adult students encounter new material can create situations in their classroom that will take advantage of this process, even as they also seek ways to engage their adult learners in achieving synthesis and evaluation on a regular basis. Concurrently, adult learners typically express a

FIGURE 6.2

Outcomes

Competence	**Outcome**
Knowledge	Remember bits of information, terminologies, techniques, specific usage
Comprehension	Understand a communication so that it can be summarized or explained
Application	Use what you know in a concrete (i.e., real life) situation
Analysis	Dissect the subject matter, explain how the parts fit together
Synthesis	Put the pieces back together in a new way, collecting information from many sources, create new insights
Evaluation	Judge the value of the subject matter for a specific purpose

preference for learning situations and environments that promote higher level learning because it enhances the entire learning experience.

IT'S NOT EXPERIENCE, IT'S WHAT YOU LEARN FROM THE EXPERIENCE

A hallmark of the adult learner movement has long been the utilization of some form of prior learning assessment. Formally, its earliest manifestation can be traced to more than 30 years ago (Whitaker, 1989), though the principles that it embodies are also a byproduct from the overall assessment movement that began to define best practices in higher education slightly earlier than that. Indeed, although various regional accrediting bodies place different levels of emphasis on assessment, they all tend to agree that this is an essential portion of the academy's strategy to achieve quality in the 21st century among adult programs. Consequently, it is obvious that this activity is widely supported. However, some groups have recently taken a special interest in adult learning since prior learning assessment often provides a unique opportunity for students to match the learning they have obtained from various life and job experiences with specific courses in the curriculum. When done correctly, this can significantly enhance an adult learning program. On the other hand, there are a number of unfortunate instances where the process has been compromised. Indeed, in the worst examples, some institutions have used the inappropriate granting of prior learning credits as an unethical and unscrupulous way to attract students. This practice, in turn, has often reduced the credibility of adult programs in general, though when done right, the granting of prior learning credit can be as rigorous and challenging as any intellectual activity on a campus.

CLEP, ACE, and Excelsior

Although creating portfolios to display how their learning experiences match up with specific course objectives tends to be the primary focus for many adult programs, there are other options available to adults that enable them to register credit for knowledge gained outside the formal classroom. The following is a brief summary of the most utilized sources that grant credit for college-level learning without necessarily having to take courses.

The College Level Examination Program (CLEP) offers specific subject examinations in areas ranging from accounting to western civilization as well as five general examinations in English composition, mathematics, humanities, natural science, and social science. The examinations are administered through the College Board, cost approximately $50 per exam, and are available at more than 1,400 test centers at colleges and universities. Information regarding registration, online exams, and other details is available at www.collegeboard.com/clep. Different schools have different guidelines regarding what CLEP credits they will accept, but once a student has successfully completed the exam, CLEP keeps the scores on file for 20 years, so students are not confined where they may apply their credits.

The American Council on Education (ACE) offers college credit directly for educational training completed through business and industry, the armed services, or government organizations. ACE evaluates a wide range of business and military training for college and its equivalencies, and keeps records of all individuals who have participated in these programs. Typically, students are asked to have ACE transcripts sent directly to the school where they expect to matriculate. More information about this program can be obtained at www.acenet.edu.

Excelsior College Examinations (formerly Regents College Examinations) offer more than 40 exams, with more than half for upper-level college credit. These exams are accepted for credit at nearly 1,000 universities and colleges worldwide and are offered free to all military personnel. There are five general areas from which the exams are drawn: associate degrees for arts and sciences, business, education, and nursing, and a baccalaureate degree for nursing. There is a rather wide range of fees associated with the examinations. Excelsior College offers a number of resources available to assist students in preparing for the exam. More information about this program can be obtained at www.excelsior.edu.

Each school is likely to have its own version of what is acceptable for an adult to submit in order to demonstrate his or her knowledge, but almost all schools offer some version of these opportunities for adult learners.

Licensure

Regardless of what options are utilized, the expectation remains similar: adults earning college credit for what they know. Although there are some instances where the prior learning credit is generalized (that is, a student may obtain a certain number of credit hours applied to general course work because they have a pilot's license or serve as a registered nurse, for instance), there is no standardized approach to this situation. Therefore, an adult learner who has been licensed as an RN may receive a number of credit hours automatically from one school while another school may not give him or her any automatic credit at all. At that school, the student would likely still have prior learning assessment to assist him or her with attaining credit for knowledge gained.

Prior Learning Assessment

Through the exhaustive efforts of the Council for Adult and Experiential Learning (CAEL), a set of standards was created to assure quality in assessing learning for credit. Since these standards have been published, CAEL has continued to disperse training, support research, and offer publications to promote their appropriate use and application. Unfortunately, there are many faculty and administrators who are still unaware of the existence of these standards, and thus are likely to assume that procedures related to this activity lack rigor. In order to rectify that misconception, the standards are offered here with the kind permission of CAEL (Figure 6.3).

In recent years, there has been a tendency among many adult programs to offer credit for life experience, not the learning gained from that experience. As indicated above, this practice is contrary to the general principles that define quality prior learning assessment and the assignment

FIGURE 6.3

Ten Standards

Academic Standards

1) Credit should be awarded only for learning and not for experience.
2) College credit should be awarded only for college-level learning.
3) Credit should be awarded only for learning that has a balance, appropriate to the subject, between theory and practical application.
4) The determination of competence levels and credit awards must be made by appropriate subject matter and academic experts.
5) Credit should be appropriate to the academic context in which it is accepted.

Administrative Standards

6) Credit awards and their transcript entries should be monitored to avoid giving credit twice for the same learning.
7) Policies and procedures applied to assessment, including provision for appeal, should be fully disclosed and prominently available.
8) Fees charged for assessment should be based on the services performed in the process and not determined by the amount of credit awarded.
9) All personnel involved in the assessment of learning should receive adequate training for the functions they perform, and there should be provision for their continued professional development.
10) Assessment programs should be regularly monitored, reviewed, evaluated, and revised as needed to reflect changes in the needs being served and in the state of assessment arts.

of credit. In fact, there are a number of unethical and sometimes unscrupulous initiatives associated with this practice. Because so many adults have a profound need to complete their studies as quickly as possible, some schools have dangled a wholesale approach to granting prior learning credit as an inducement to attract students. In other cases, this approach is not offered to newly admitted students but instead as they near completion. For instance, a 35-year-old student with ten years' work experience in a business might receive 30 "life experience credits" to be applied to general elective credits automatically without benefit of any serious screening or preparation of portfolio. Once again, although these activities only represent a distinct minority among adult programs, their practice tends to undermine the credibility of adult learning initiatives in general.

In response to these concerns most of the regional accrediting bodies have drawn specific guidelines regarding appropriate practices associated with prior learning assessment. The Higher Learning Commission of the North Central Association approved the following policy statement:

1) Make clear basic principles and values held by the institution regarding credit for prior learning.

2) Provide explicit guidelines as to what is considered college-level learning.

3) Make clear that credit can be awarded only for demonstrated college-level *learning,* not for experience per se.

4) Specify, as clearly and unambiguously as possible, the standards of acceptable performance in each academic area.

5) Specify what form the claim for credit should take, e.g., course equivalent, competency list.

6) Ensure that evaluation of learning is undertaken by appropriately qualified persons.

7) Indicate the appropriate form such as semester hours, course units, etc., the evaluator's credit recommendation should take.

8) Specify which degree requirements may be met by prior learning.

9) Specify how credit for prior learning will be recorded.

10) Define and articulate roles and responsibilities of all persons connected with the assessment process.

11) Develop procedures to monitor and assure fair and consistent treatment of students.

12) Develop clearly stated assessment policies and descriptive information for students, faculty, administrators, and external sources.

13) Include provisions for periodic reevaluation of policies and procedures for assessing learning and awarding credit.

14) Advise students that the institution cannot guarantee the transferability of prior learning credits to another institution.

15) Develop evaluation procedures of overall prior learning assessment programs to ensure quality. (Middle States Commission on Higher Education, 1996, pp. 6–7)

Adult learners seeking credit for what they have learned through their life and career experiences are the natural extension of the learning process they bring with them into the classroom. Although this element may be unique to the adult learner, the longstanding existence of many of these programs and the level of safeguards that have been built into them suggest that they are valid.

Cynthia may not be a typical adult learner, but neither is she so unique when it comes to her experience and background. If it's a challenge for the typical adult learner to attend college, imagine how difficult it is for someone like Cynthia who is perceived as highly successful in her business community. Having the level of power and leadership experience she possesses may present special problems when she walks into the classroom, but the situation also helps us understand how she is likely to process the information she is exposed to. While much of the material she encounters is likely to be new, Cynthia has experienced such a broad range of information as she has worked her way up the corporate ladder that almost everything she encounters in the classroom will be colored and affected by her background. In fact, students like Cynthia sometime face the additional problem of knowing more about material covered in class than the instructor. Occasionally, adult learners can share their own experiences to help illustrate a learning moment when the professor is willing to give the student the opportunity. Learning centered attitudes in the classroom are particularly conducive to generating this type of meaningful dialogue.

Case Study: Cynthia

Cynthia's roots were humble, though you would never think that now as she sits in her office on the 30th floor of one of the nation's largest banks.

Cynthia's story is a female version of Horatio Alger—she has worked extremely hard all her life and has always been determined to work her way up the corporate ladder. Anyone who meets Cynthia quickly notes that there is, indeed, a bright fire that burns in her that will not be denied. She is proud when someone describes her as ambitious.

Her story begins with her earliest childhood years where, in a rural section in one of the southern states, she helped contribute to the small business her family ran. In fact, there was no time until she graduated from high school that she ever had a break from the work. Much of what Cynthia did at that time was manual and unskilled labor, encompassing long hours and physical hardship. But these experiences also prepared her for her future and the better life she envisioned for herself.

Cynthia was determined to make something more of her life than merely remain where she grew up or work in the family business. As a result, she moved to the big city immediately after graduating from high school. Her first job was an entry-level position for the bank she still works for today. Twenty-two years later, still applying the incredible work ethic that had always defined her, while also having ample opportunities to demonstrate how bright she was, she had managed to work herself into her present executive position of associate vice president. In her mind, each step up the corporate ladder helped convince her that there was no limit to how far she could advance. Indeed, her mentors had helped reinforce that notion on many occasions as well.

Therefore, she was downright shocked when she came into her annual performance evaluation with Brad, her boss, who carefully explained that the bank was introducing a new policy for upper management: "No degree equals no advancement" was to be the official policy from this point onward (with no "grandfather" clause for those few individuals like Cynthia who had been with the company for a long time). In fact, Brad explained that this was a classic glass ceiling situation: "The company is no longer willing to offer raises or promotions to any executive who doesn't possess a degree. Of course, I'm still impressed with your work and, assuming that you are willing to seek a degree with the same diligence and energy you have applied during your career here, I will try to provide you with as much support as possible to accomplish that goal."

Although Cynthia was initially stunned, she quickly researched her options and selected a school that had a solid reputation among the banks in the city. She was also careful to determine that the school offered the sort of adult-friendly opportunities that appealed to her: maximum scheduling options with accelerated courses at the core of the system; a high degree of convenience regarding accessibility, parking, services, and support; and (perhaps most important) a highly reputable prior learning assessment program. Once she successfully completed her first four courses, she was able to take the prior learning course. This ultimately enabled her to gain 39 credit hours toward her degree based on the learning she had acquired from her past experiences and the portfolio she created to demonstrate her knowledge. With nearly one-third of her requirements fulfilled in this manner, the goal of completing a degree didn't seem nearly as much of a challenge.

As Cynthia moves further into her degree she has had to redistribute some of her efforts in the workplace in order to meet classroom demands. The classes have proven to have a surprising impact on her life as she continually finds herself filtering the information she learns in class through her own experiences. While this process has often proven gratifying—affirming some action she might have taken without even necessarily having the theoretical foundation upon which to build her actions—she has also encountered a number of instances where she is now able to gain greater insights and understanding. Cynthia constantly reflects on her own growth as a result of this process.

At the same time, she is finding that her educational experiences are also having an unanticipated benefit when it comes to her career. Recently, there have been some opportunities to either directly apply what she has been learning in the classroom or to work with one of the teams in her class on a problem that, once they have obtained the solution, she can generalize back to her work situation. Finally, there is one additional, unforeseen benefit Cynthia has recently discovered about her school experience: She and her niece will be graduating on the same day this spring (though at different institutions) as the first two members of her family to ever graduate from college.

●●●●●

Conclusion

As I listen to faculty members speak about adult learners, I am often impressed with how many of them clearly care about their students. I have seen many examples of professors—regardless whether they are full-time or adjunct—making extraordinary efforts on behalf of their students. However, not all faculty members share that sense of caring. One common-sense issue relating to what adult learners bring to the campus needs to be addressed before this chapter concludes. In some ways, the issue relates to some of the characteristics covered in Chapter 2: the need for respect and the importance of mattering.

These themes emerge repeatedly when speaking with students who articulate their dissatisfaction with faculty members. On many occasions, adult learners will relate their perception that an instructor is indifferent to the time constraints, responsibilities, and obligations that tend to make their lives different from traditional students. Many are quite specific and emphatic that they are not seeking special privileges or consideration. Often, these are individuals who have achieved a level of success in their lives but feel as though they are powerless when they enter the classroom. Admittedly, this kind of situation can be subjective, but with open discussion, it is possible to confirm the students' reports as well. (There are some instances where faculty members have no idea how the students are reading their behavior, and so after a conversation, they become genuinely anxious to address the problem. But I have also encountered some faculty members who are less flexible in their approach to adult learners.)

Some faculty members may use their position as a bully pulpit and their authority as a weapon. Adult learners are likely to have little tolerance or patience for such behavior in the classroom. Although there are degrees of this behavior—from very subtle to extremely overt—two indicators usually confirm the reality of this situation: 1) repeated complaints from numerous students, and 2) the use of evaluation instruments or exit interviews.

The first sign of an instructor who lacks respect for adult learners is a pattern of reports to an administrator from numerous sources. When a number of adults, sometimes from different classes or sections, provide independent details concerning a faculty member who seems to undermine the importance of mattering or respecting adult learners, it is usually a "where there's smoke there's fire" situation. On the other hand, because adult learners can be manipulative, it's a good idea to start with a conversation with the faculty member to determine his or her perspective. As previously indicated, many faculty members merely need better faculty development, from accelerated learning issues to meaningful insights. On the other hand, a conversation at this time sometimes reveals a faculty member for whom teaching adult learners simply doesn't provide a good fit for either party. But I'm convinced that most adult programs could be significantly improved by simply offering regular development sessions on a series of topics for all affected faculty.

One final strategy I have used to determine whether faculty members are interacting with adult learners appropriately is to carefully examine all evaluations (though in some instances, faculty members are not obligated to evaluate all courses) or offer exit interviews with graduating students. Sometimes when there are unpleasant situations in the classroom, it reaches a level where the student is reluctant to say anything at the time for fear of retribution. Clearly, this becomes a trust issue, but even after the course is complete, administrators don't always hear about some of the serious problems that might take place in the classroom. However, when you ask these students to summarize their experiences in general and then to be specific about "the good, the bad, and the ugly," they are sometimes ready to reveal incidents that might never have surfaced otherwise. Of course, the students are always quick to identify those faculty and staff members who provided stellar support, but by asking for details concerning disappointing circumstances, you are already indicating your desire to help your program achieve its full potential.

For the most part, I have found that faculty members who are stimulated by working with adult learners are likely to make the classroom a dynamic place. At a previous school, one instructor offered a sequence of courses. Each class met in the morning from 6:00 to 7:30 twice weekly. The instructor always arrived early, provided bagels and juice and interacted with the students before the beginning of class as if they were all old friends. However, once the class began, the same instructor became a taskmaster, working the class hard and ensuring that everyone had completed the work assigned. The students loved this instructor, which is why, even at that terrible time of the morning, the courses were always fully enrolled. In many ways, he fully understood the components described in this chapter. Indeed, this is the prototype for any instructor seeking to be successful with adult learners.

REFERENCES

Middle States Commission on Higher Education. (1996). *Assessing prior learning for credit.* Philadelphia, PA: Author.

Vella, J. (2002, Spring). Quantum learning: Teaching as dialogue. *New Directions for Adult and Continuing Education, 93,* 73–83.

Whitaker, U. (1989). *Assessing learning: Standards, principles & procedures.* Philadelphia, PA: Council for Adult and Experiential Learning.

7

Senior Citizens: The New Adult Learner

Overview

Until recently, the notion of senior citizens having a significant place as students on the campus probably seemed incongruous with the academy's mission. But today, one of the fastest growing demographic groups in America is comprised of senior citizens. Nationwide, more people will turn 65 in the next 20 years than ever before. At one time, this age represented the end of their life expectancy. Now, a newly retired individual can look forward to a lifestyle that often prominently includes learning.

This chapter looks at the wide range of noncredit options colleges and universities are offering this population and the reasons why. It also examines a relatively new phenomenon in the academy: senior citizens pursuing for-credit courses, certificates, and degrees.

Introduction

On college campuses across the nation, the concept of lifelong learning is beginning to take shape as something more than mere high-minded rhetoric. Now, the notion of "birth to post-retirement," "cradle to rocker," or the more explicit "cradle to death" learning opportunities, with the college or university as the central learning resource for an expanded community, is becoming more of a reality. A growing number of schools have begun to envision lifelong learning as an important and integral part of their mission, as reflected by the inclusion of this phrase in an increasing number of updated mission statements. But despite the inclusive language, few schools have taken any meaningful actions to address the learning needs of student populations at the extreme ends of the life cycle. This is especially true when it comes to so-called senior citizens.

But this is not a demographic that will eventually disappear. In fact, demographic projections suggest that the category that includes those individuals who expect to turn 65 within the next ten years is the fastest-growing and largest segment of the US population. This chapter will examine why it makes sense for schools to determine strategies to actively include this group in their outreach and what those strategies might involve.

Even when institutional response to senior adult learners may be largely pragmatic, it extends beyond considerations of simple income margin and embraces an aspect of diversity that touches one of society's final, but more powerful, underrepresented frontiers: ageism. Therefore, the post-65 age segment of the learning continuum is particularly noteworthy because it represents the potential for powerful intellectual contributions, it satisfies inclusion of an overlooked minority, and it offers significant financial implications for the academy. Not only are senior adult learners worthy in terms of what they bring into the classroom, but because of their advanced age and the level of financial stability many have achieved, they are more likely to demonstrate their appreciation to colleges who have provided quality learning opportunities for them sooner than most of their classmates. There is ample and growing evidence that a major segment of this population is seeking a diverse range of learning options for themselves and that they believe higher education should be their primary source to accommodate that need. As college presidents come to better understand these implications, more of them are likely to seek meaningful learning outlets for this special population on their campus.

Ford Knew More Than Automobiles

Today's senior citizen (65 years or older) is not the same sort of person Americans have encountered in past generations. In part, this is a reflection of longevity: More individuals are living longer than ever before. Furthermore, the lifestyle of these individuals is notably different when compared with previous populations. Older adults approach their retirement years with an expectation and even a commitment to staying busy—physically, emotionally, spiritually, and intellectually. As a result of their longevity as well as how we perceive them in general, many senior citizens are seeking strategies for maintaining meaningful and fulfilling lives, frequently through some form of learning activity.

To paraphrase a comment attributed to Henry Ford, age is more a state of mind than a physical condition. We are reminded of this based on what we see on television and what we are likely to encounter in our daily life. It may be reassuring that this homey observation is grounded by solid research. In a book by Bronte (as cited in Canja, 2002) she says:

> There is no inevitable biological decline either of the brain or of the mind. The available evidence seems to indicate that if you stop using your facilities—at any age—they (sic) may suffer, but as a result of disuse—not chronological age. Creativity is not just the privilege of youth. (p. 29)

Each day brings new confirmation that the majority of retired adults have already internalized this message, as reflected (among other things) by surging enrollment figures in programs designed for them. Furthermore, senior citizens have more lifestyle options than ever before. As a result, older adults also have more freedom and independence than their ancestors. With the so-called graying of America and its rising mean age, many rules and assumptions have been called into question in our culture, resulting in more of an "all things are possible" mentality. So with the proliferation of diverse educational options, senior citizens have learned to see all educational pathways accessible to them, whether the learning is casual or part of an advanced degree.

Post-65-year-olds are everywhere in our society and yet, we have probably not fully adjusted to their presence, their needs, or how they are likely to influence our future. In part, their ubiquity is due to two factors: 1) they tend to lead dramatically more active lives so that they are more visible, and 2) their numbers are greater than ever before. As a result, they permeate all aspects of our culture and are a greater part of our consciousness than ever before. (For example, turn to television commercials and note how many of them are directed to this generation, as well as how many use actors from this generation. When compared to the past, this is a sea change in practice.) Furthermore, they are already better educated, have greater buying power, and are physically more fit than any of their predecessors. In addition, their willingness to integrate technology into their lives is especially notable. The levels of independence they have been able to gain as a result of technology is opening up new vistas beyond anyone's wildest imagination. Consequently, their lives may often seem like they are based on science fiction even to them, since these dramatic and dynamic lifestyle changes in American culture have taken place over a relatively short period of time. And while the nature and conditions of changes related to this population actually extend far beyond the few examples cited here, their voting impact (especially in regard to state institutions) and their ability to offer substantial financial patronage (particularly, though not exclusively, in regard to private schools) may eventually hold the greatest educational implications. Their growing influence at the ballot box is only beginning to be recognized but it is considered likely to directly influence many aspects of life in the 21st century in ways never experienced in the past as this population achieves a virtual gerontocracy. In short, this is a population that the academy cannot afford to ignore in the future.

Any college or university that does not intentionally plan to integrate some form of learning opportunities for senior adult learners into its strategic plan may regret the oversight. This generation is already giving Henry Ford's comments credence and they will inevitably continue to do so in the future, reflecting their lifelong commitment to and interest in learning.

"But how," you may ask, "does this generation relate to the issue of adult learning as it has been discussed in this book so far?" After all, adult learners who are 65 or older don't appear to have either the vocational need or other incentives to motivate them to seek degrees, certificates, or other for-credit endeavors. Although the majority of this population may not opt to take for-credit courses for any purpose, there has always been a small number of senior citizens seeking this kind of experience. Now, however, with the greater opportunity and changing profile of members of this generation, that number will inevitably increase.

When it comes to taking classes with younger students, this generation can be even more explicit about their reasons for continuing their studies. Members of this generation are often outspoken when they express why they are actively seeking learning experiences in a cross-generational, age-integrated classroom. When asked, most students 65 or older are likely to reply that, "being around young students provides fresh, new perspectives" which, they often contend, adds to their energy and sense of enthusiasm. In other words, they are seeking the full extent of what Ford envisioned, spiritually, physically, and intellectually.

The Interactive Classroom Takes On a Whole New Meaning

Although higher education began designing educational programs to respond to the needs of senior citizens as early as 1963, the overall range of programs created specifically for this population has been modest when compared to preretired adult learners. Nonetheless, colleges and universities have begun to be more responsive in recent years (Fischer, Blazey, & Lipman, 1992). Most of the learning options available to senior learners are available through not-for-credit programs. However, recent advances, particularly in technology, now make distance-learning opportunities a great equalizer for senior adult learners in the early 21st century. Not only is age an insignificant consideration for enrollment in distance courses, but other factors that might serve to prohibit their enrollment (such as a lack of mobility, infirmities, threatening weather conditions) are neutralized by this format. And since many distance courses are designed to be asynchronous (allowing the student to participate according to their own schedule rather than a predetermined schedule for everyone in the class), the elderly student may enjoy the additional benefit of working at their own pace while taking as much time as they need to complete their studies. On the other hand, the majority of older adult students seek to learn in a group setting among others because they particularly value the socialization aspect of their learning. That is, part of what older students gain from their learning experiences can be attributed to social interaction and the stimulation this population gains from that experience.

The majority of senior citizens are still utilizing real-time, in-class learning opportunities. Although they are participating in all aspects of higher education learning, the majority of these students are enrolled in not-for-credit courses since their pursuit of knowledge is on a more fundamental level rather than the more formal pursuit of grades. For the most part, these students are learning for the pure sake of learning. That is not to say, however, that their learning can in any way be described as passive. The proliferation of learning choices designed specifically to meet the needs of older Americans ensures that classrooms can expect more senior citizens each year. The characteristics of any adult learner apply to this generation, but there is anecdotal evidence that many of these students become more fully involved in the classroom, perhaps because so many of these learners have reached a stage in their life where they tend to be more direct and outspoken. The general frameworks for classes that most appeal to older adult learners are described below, distinguished by their for-credit and not-for-credit status.

Not-for-Credit Courses

Among successful not-for-credit programs designed specifically for post-65-year-old learners, most are based on a comprehensive yet less rigorous learning experience. This is not to suggest that such courses need to be overly simplified nor trivialized. Indeed, many deserve to be considered rigorous (particularly because it is not unusual for the courses to be taught by current or retired professors), but the learning tends to be highly interactive while the pace is likely to be less intensive. Typically, while the main focus for these courses is on learning, the approach is often low-impact, with less formal requirements (i.e., no exams, grades, or assignments). In addition, some social dimension is more likely to be evident in the classroom. In part, this may often be attributed to the relationship between instructor and students, which tends to be less adversarial, more collegial, and more congenial. One additional aspect for many of these programs is to introduce some form of travel component into the learning experience.

Two distinctive models comprise the general format for almost all noncredit options available to seniors: 1) residency-intensive, or 2) self-directed study. The Elderhostel program (http://eh.elderhostel.org/ein), whose national office is in Boston, is typical of the first example, where participants travel to a site and enroll in one or two courses for approximately one week. During this "term," the students live either in hotel rooms or in dormitories (less likely). (A new version of this model has utilized cruise ships as the location for both study and living.) Although Elderhostel began with courses offered almost exclusively on college campuses, the program has evolved so that, while the programs are usually still sponsored or overseen by colleges or universities, they are often likely to take place off-campus. Furthermore, in many instances the curriculum is designed to capitalize on the location.

Elderhostel is a nonprofit, self-supporting program that was first introduced in 1975. Its modest beginning (five sites with a total enrollment of 220 students) belies its present success. In 2001, Elderhostel enrolled more than a quarter-million students in over 10,000 programs taking place in more than 100 countries.

For instance, a course offered in Louisville, Kentucky, might build a visit to Churchill Downs into one of its class activities along with discussions of the local history, culture, and other topics that represent the high points of the area. Like any good learning experience, students are encouraged to extend their learning beyond the classroom in the program—in this case, by the very design and location of the course. While the initial learning may take place through the instructor, students often interact among themselves during their "free time" to promote greater self-directed learning. As a result, courses often require a greater level of flexibility since an ad hoc aspect that comes out of the students' interests or self-directed study may arise in the middle of the course.

The Elderhostel programs have become increasingly sophisticated with a virtual smorgasbord of choices and options. For instance, they provide an extensive catalog that includes international travel opportunities with built-in classes to heighten the overall experience. The Elderhostel program offers courses throughout the nation, year round.

The self-directed, conventional format draws its inspiration largely from for-credit college courses, but is modified to meet slightly different objectives. Unlike Elderhostel, there are numerous local programs that tend to be more independent and responsive to regional needs in how they offer learning opportunities to senior citizens. Although these programs are often quite distinctive, they are likely to share some common characteristics. For example, many of the programs tend to be autonomous, with their own faculty, schedule, leadership, and infrastructure. Many offer self-directed study opportunities that enable students to determine among themselves the nature and direction of their course work.

Although many programs utilize retired faculty, current college faculty, or experts from relevant fields, some are designed to use a moderator rather than a faculty member. Often in this context, the group makes decisions regarding the topic, format, and member-responsibilities or assignments. In this application, the class may determine weekly readings for discussions; guest speakers; and the nature, criteria, and/or the order of class member reports. Under these circumstances, the learning really is self-directed with a greater focus upon the individual needs of the class members.

The other format common to this category draws more directly from the academy where an instructor leads the class. Typically, the courses in this format run from five to eight weeks with each class lasting approximately one and one-half hours. Although there are almost as many variations as there are programs, they all share the benefits of being available to the immediate community, often (though not always) with a modest membership fee structure as well. In fact, the tuition for this format is as diverse as the various programs, ranging from minimal to fairly expensive. Many colleges or universities sustain or even underwrite the self-directed conventional format by offering special consideration to alumni—a group the school may have a vested interest in supporting.

Structurally, some of these programs are fully autonomous. Some even own their building and/or maintain a separate budget and bank account from the host institution. Others rely heavily on the college or university to sustain or underwrite aspects of their existence. The underlying philosophy differs from program to program as well. For instance, some programs are based on inclusion, with an objective that all qualified (i.e., retired) members of the community's population be able to participate. Such programs typically offer classes at an extremely modest tuition (often, less than $25 per course). On the other hand, some programs prefer to be highly selective. In addition to prohibitive tuitions, they may also restrict enrollments by more stringent admission policies or use other barriers to control their membership. Such programs, however, appear to be in the minority.

For-Credit Courses

More senior adult learners are seeking for-credit courses as an alternative for their learning needs than ever before. For the most part, these older students seek to pursue their studies as a college student with either a certificate or degree as their objective. Still others are apt to enroll in an occasional course with no formal structure to their long-range plans. While the number of degree completion or certificate programs designed specifically for senior citizens is still rather limited, many community colleges and some state schools offer courses to senior adult learners either tuition-free or at significantly reduced cost. It is likely that more schools will be intentional about these choices in the future as the potential for attracting more students from this population increases.

In some instances, these students may already possess a degree but since their studies are not vocationally oriented, their motives are quite different from their classmates. Although reasons abound for older adult learners to explain their desire to complete a degree or certificate, most can be distilled into two distinctive explanations. Many older students feel they have something to prove, either to themselves or to others. Under the right circumstances, this can be an extremely strong motivator. At the same time, others seek completion of a degree or certificate as a metaphor for an important journey. "I'm much more interested in what I do along the way rather than focusing on getting there" pretty much summarizes their sentiments. These reasons confirm a study by the American Association of Retired Persons (2000) that examined why older adults want to learn:

- To keep up with what's going on in the world (93%)
- For their own spiritual or personal growth (92%)
- For the simple joy of learning something new (91%) (p. 2)

Regardless of their reasons, substantial and significant numbers of senior adult learners are looking to take their place in the college classroom. While they might have been a rare exception at one time, their numbers will continue to grow with the academy of the 21st century, in part as a constant factor within a surging population (that is, even if the proportion of older adult learners remains the same, their number will inevitably grow as their demographic increases), but also in response to institutional efforts. For instance, in 1989, Dychtwald and Flower noted, "Nationwide, more than a thousand colleges now actively encourage people over 65 to take classes for credit, and more than 120 schools have adopted special programs just for the older learner" (p. 149).

Although this population is not likely to ever represent a major portion of the total campus enrollment, there is ample evidence that their intentional inclusion in strategic plans may prove beneficial to the institution. While a portion of the benefits of creating programs for senior adult learners may be attributed to potential increases in the endowment and other fundraising efforts, the significant beneficiaries are likely to be those traditional-aged students who share a classroom with them. Not only do they have the opportunity to gain meaningful historical perspectives, often from firsthand accounts, but their lives are likely to be enriched in many other ways from this exposure. In other words, opening the classroom to "retired" learners offers a campus a series of win/win solutions.

● ● ● ● ●

There is a quality of purity that many older adult learners bring with them into the classroom. In part, this is due to their purpose for learning: They tend to seek learning for its joy and satisfaction rather than to impart any vocational or achievement considerations onto the experience. Furthermore, they are typically enthusiastic learners, often taking in new information like children, with pleasure and delight. Doris is a composite of many classmates in her generation. In this country, they still form a largely invisible student body when considered from the perspective of the majority of the academy's faculty and administrators, but they are a formidable group and have the potential for making a significant impact on 21st century campuses everywhere.

CASE STUDY: DORIS

Three years ago, Doris retired from her position as an administrative assistant in an office where she had worked for 40 years. When her coworkers asked about her plans she always replied with the same response: "I don't know what I'm going to do yet but I won't be inactive or just watching television!" Shortly before her retirement began, she received a flyer from the local college, Laverne-Clark College (L-C), offering short, noncredit courses for senior citizens. She went to the introductory orientation and, "The rest," she says, "is history." She enrolled in her first two classes ("Jazz History" and "Assassinated Presidents") the same day.

Although there was no grade, exam, or even assignment, Doris found herself excited to be among a large group of her peers, all actively seeking to learn new things, be introduced to new ideas, and enjoy the pure pleasure of gaining knowledge and growing at their own pace and volition. The campus group that had designed the program, Learning Explorations For Seniors (LExFS), had insisted from its inception five years ago that all courses be substantial and representative of college-level topics and work. When Doris first enrolled, the overall membership was already robust, most likely due to modest tuition, quality instruction, and a retiree-sensitive schedule. Doris took as many courses as she could during the three six-week terms each year. It was during her third year in the program that the college offered a new for-credit program designed especially for senior citizens.

For more than two years, L-C had discussed ways to enrich the diversity on its campus. The dean had argued that age should be considered as one of the factors for inclusiveness. "After all," he reasoned, "the objective of diversity is to broaden and enrich all perspectives, so why should age not be considered?" When L-C initiated its new program, New Vistas, one of the stated expectations required older adult learners to enroll in the same courses as any other L-C students, with the same faculty and course requirements. Although New Vistas was designed to include other underserved populations, when it came to the issue of admission requirements, it used the same criteria for senior adults as for any other adult learners at L-C. There was, however, one small added expectation: because so many of the courses had some form of computer requirement, the L-C New Vistas program required all older students to demonstrate a minimal computer proficiency, merely to protect them from being at risk. Like so many of her friends, Doris had begun using her computer to communicate with her grandchildren who were living elsewhere in the country so she already felt reasonably comfortable with the computer and, as a result, was one of the first senior citizens to enroll in New Vistas.

Doris knew from the onset that she would be unable to take a full complement of courses to qualify for "full-time" status. She tended to take two courses every term for a total of six or seven credit hours (though one ambitious semester, she did take three courses for a total of eight credit hours). Because she was not interested in a degree for any vocational purpose (she figured her career days were over), she elected to pursue a degree in liberal studies. The other feature she appreciated was the opportunity to take a prior learning assessment course. Although she felt compelled to devote all her energy during the following semester to creating the portfolio required to assess her prior learning credit (and though she missed the stimulation and student interaction from taking any other courses during this time), when she learned that she had received 24 credits, she felt that all her hard work and sacrifice had been worth it. "After all," she explained, "there was no way I could have completed 24 credits any other way during the same period of time."

Much to her surprise, Doris discovered that she really enjoyed the history and psychology courses. Often, she was able to relate topics in her textbook or in the classroom with experiences she had encountered in her lifetime first hand. Eventually, when instructors would ask students to break into groups to prepare presentations, many of the traditional students would vie with each other to have Doris join their team. For instance, when the class covered the Kennedy assassination, Doris was able to lend her own personal reactions and memories to the topic in a manner that brought the material alive to the younger members of her group. At the same time, Doris enjoyed how bright and energetic her classmates were. She was also grateful for their assistance, especially when it came to some of the more demanding computer applications. But she was most pleased by feeling that her contributions were valuable in the classroom. This was confirmed not only by her passing grades but also by her classmates' inclusiveness.

By the time Doris was ready to graduate, L-C had admitted 28 New Vistas senior citizens. Among the four who had been admitted at the same time as Doris, three had remained. Each of the 28 students occasionally remarked that while the work seemed very demanding, this was probably the most exciting and gratifying time of their life. Doris was particularly mindful of those feelings on May 13 of the past year when her classmates gave her a standing ovation as she crossed the stage during her commencement.

As a bonus, L-C has hired Doris to serve as a part-time campus liaison with the noncredit program designed for senior citizens. Doris recently remarked, "This is where I originally began and perhaps I can assist some of my colleagues in this program to pursue the same path I took." The college is hoping the same thing.

● ● ● ● ●

Conclusion

Convincing colleges and universities to purposefully expand their student body to include senior citizens can be daunting, especially in environments where more conventional adult learners (i.e., 25 to 55 years old) may not yet be fully absorbed or accepted into the culture of the institution. But for those schools willing to support older learners, the benefits can hold special promises and rewards. This is especially true in regions where the demographic distribution by age may be heavily skewed (i.e., areas or states where disproportionate numbers of senior citizens move for retirement are one such group). But whether the institution feels compelled to integrate this population by virtue of pragmatic considerations or out of simple recognition that this is a group of learners that deserve inclusion, the academy will probably be slow to respond to or support such an initiative.

When I came to Baldwin-Wallace College (B-W) in 1999, the school had already begun a noncredit learning institute for senior citizens six years previously. This was one of the first groups of constituents I sought to establish a dialogue with since I had already experienced some exciting programs with older learners at previous institutions. (In fact, I had helped establish a beginner's band for senior citizens that continued to serve as a model wherever I have spoken or written about integrating older learners into the campus community.) What I encountered at B-W was a solid program with approximately 250 members. Just two years later, the membership had swelled to more than 600. I hasten to add that the reasons for this increase were in large part due to a wonderful steering committee, comprised of dedicated members and strong leadership from the group's presidents.

One of the most telling moments took place early in my first year when I asked the steering committee to clarify its mission and create an informal strategic plan. As a result of the discussion that evolved from this simple expectation, the steering committee arrived at an epiphany: "We want to attract as many members as possible." It was exciting to see everyone come to a common conclusion about this issue. This simple revelation was then reinforced among the membership and everyone was soon working on achieving that single objective. From then on, the new members grew exponentially.

During the next three years, I made a concentrated effort to teach at least one course a year for this group. My final two courses averaged an enrollment of about 110 students each. I was thrilled by the level of interest demonstrated by my students, their willingness to take copious notes (despite not having either exams or grades to worry about), their enthusiasm at bringing related materials to class, or even buying supplemental materials so they could discover more about the topics on their own. I quickly realized that these students epitomized the very best of what professors always seek in their students regardless of their age or other circumstances. I found teaching these students to be extremely gratifying and the courses were more dynamic as a result of their heightened interaction.

What I may not have anticipated was how soon I would apply what I had learned from my experiences in these classes. During my second year at B-W, I proposed a degree completion model designed explicitly for senior citizens. My division had polled the members of the noncredit group (at this time they had a mailing list of over 1,000) by sketching out what we envisioned. We then asked what their level of interest might be. When we concluded the survey, more than 200 potential students had indicated their desire to participate in the degree completion program. It was with this knowledge that we made a proposal for the Century Program. However, I was unprepared for the number of faculty who expressed serious concerns and reluctance to teach this population. Many faculty members suggested that they felt intimidated to teach "someone as old as my grandparent." I am convinced that this is a genuine problem for a small portion of the faculty, but it's not a compelling enough reason to turn away this population from a college-level learning experience.

As part of my response, I framed those qualities I had experienced directly with senior learners in my recent classes. I wondered aloud about all the desirable characteristics I had observed among older learners: how, for instance, the members of the senior citizen beginner's band had applied themselves with a level of focus and commitment that could only be described as professional. Indeed, I was more struck by that attitude in all applications I had encountered—how serious they were about the whole thing—than by their scholarship or their musicianship (which wasn't extraordinary other than the fact that the average age of the 35-piece ensemble was over 75). And while I agreed with the faculty members about their concerns that occasionally a senior learner might dominate a class discussion or make a lecture more challenging because the student might interject his or her personal experiences into the topic, I also expressed my confidence in their classroom management skills. And I further suggested that once they saw these students as rich resources to draw upon for a wider range of perspectives than they would otherwise ever encounter, they were likely to welcome these students into their classroom.

Although the enrollment for this special program remains modest, it was never about numbers in the first place. It seems to me that colleges and universities have an obligation to respond to the needs of every part of their community. I believe the real role for the academy is to be a rich resource for learners of all ages—to provide learning opportunities and to assist anyone seeking greater knowledge. As for the bottom-line thinkers among you, I can assure you that there is probably no more vocal or supportive group imaginable than those members of the B-W noncredit program for seniors. They are incredibly proud of their affiliation with the school and would do anything for the institution. As their program has increased in success, they have turned over a greater portion of their proceeds to the college. In addition, they also contribute an impressive amount to the Division of Lifelong Learning in order to support scholarships for adult learners. But it is not just the direct monetary benefit that makes this relationship so worthwhile.

B-W will probably never know exactly how many traditional-aged students have enrolled as a result of their grandparents' influence, but I'm prepared to say that the number is substantial. Therefore, it is the level of continuity that our senior adult learners supply the institution that may be their most valuable contribution. They bring the words "lifelong learning" alive in many unimaginable ways.

References

American Association of Retired Persons. (2000, July). *AARP survey on lifelong learning: Executive summary.* Retrieved April 6, 2002, from http://research.aarp.org/general/lifelong_1.html

Canja, E. T. (2002, Spring). Lifelong learning: Challenges & opportunities. *CAEL Forum and News,* 26–29.

Dychtwald, K., & Flower, J. (1989). *Age wave: The challenges and opportunities of an aging America.* Los Angeles, CA: Jeremy P. Tarcher, Inc.

Fischer, R. B., Blazey, M. L., & Lipman, H. T. (Eds.). (1992). *Students of the third age.* New York, NY: Macmillan.

PART THREE

INSTITUTIONAL RESPONSES TO THE ADULT LEARNER

8

What Adults Need in Their Learning Environment

Overview

When it comes to addressing the needs of adult learners, many colleges and universities make a number of fundamental mistakes. Research indicates that adult learners are a distinct population and that their needs are unique. Often, however, schools use a cookie-cutter approach that doesn't separate out or even recognize these special needs. Furthermore, adult learner needs span all facets of the academy—from curricular to support and from scheduling formats to registration options.

On the other hand, understanding these needs enables the institution to position itself to maximize its target audience. In today's highly competitive market, the responsive college or university is likely to have an advantage. From a learning perspective, research has confirmed that proper andragogy (teaching principles for the adult learner) is one way to optimize instruction for adults. Successful schools that seek to focus their efforts on adult learners are more likely to be flexible, responsive, and accessible. Finally, faculty members are a crucial linchpin for the institution to achieve its full potential when it comes to the adult learner.

Introduction

Although some members of the campus community may continue to resist the notion, one of the most dramatic shifts the academy has experienced in the early 21st century has focused on how it thinks about students. Perhaps there is a better word than "customer" but it does capture a school's relationship with adult learners. Given the unparalleled number of options and the level of competition among the various enterprises designed to provide learning opportunities for adult learners, it is, quite frankly, naïve not to understand that these students are customers. As Chaffee (1998) indicated:

> We need to know our customers in considerable detail, including who they are, why they are here, their expectations of us, what kind of problems they have, where they turn to when they have problems, and what and how well they are learning. We need to understand the diverse types of students the institution attracts. We need to know their critical requirements of us. (p. 31)

She also notes:

> Older students, however, are increasingly aware of and vocal about their expectations. To the extent that this orientation comes to prevail, institutions that take little interest in student expectations do so at their own peril. If we do not meet student expectations, someone else will. (p. 24)

Even contemporary business perspectives have come to recognize the need for being responsive and sensitive to the needs of the customer in an ongoing fashion. According to Brendler and Vonk (2002), "Successful customer retention means getting it 'right' on an ongoing basis—based on the ability to deliver on the customer's definition of value, which is created by ongoing two-way dialogue" (p. 3).

Schmidt (1987) provides a conceptual frame from a slightly different perspective: "Client needs are the backbone of program planning and marketing, and both require an understanding of the forces at work outside the institution" (p. 36). Nonetheless, some institutions or faculty members may think about or treat adult learners the same as they do their 18- to 22-year-old students. Such a practice is obviously shortsighted and inevitably contributes to endemic problems for the adult learner population.

One need not conclude, however, that adult learners require excessive overhead or attention regarding their needs. One of the more fascinating aspects of adult learners is that, for the most part, they require less maintenance and expense than their younger classmates, but their needs are unique and distinctive. As previously indicated, they tend to be more vocal and demanding than other students, which may distort appropriate expectations in this regard. But adult learners have need of just a few essentials, primarily based on understanding.

For instance, a notable distinction between adult learners and their younger counterparts is demonstrated in the scenario below: Ask any faculty member who has taught classes with both groups and they will confirm the accuracy of the following illustration.

> **Scenario 1: Traditional Students**
> The instructor says to the class: "Well class, the work you've done today has been really productive. Believe it or not, this is all I had intended to cover, so even though the class still has ten minutes remaining, you can leave early." The class rises as one and is out of the room immediately, before the words "leave early" are fully out of the instructor's mouth.

> **Scenario 2: Adult Students**
> The instructor says to the class: "Well class, the work you've done today has been really productive. Believe it or not, this is all I had intended to cover, so even though the class still has ten minutes remaining, you can leave early." The class quickly starts complaining with variations on the following theme: "We paid our money for X number of hours in class and we want to use every minute of it. Let's find some more work we can do until the class is supposed to end."

In the first scenario, the students perceive the situation as a bonus—unanticipated free time for them to use as they see fit. In the second, the students perceive the situation as a waste of precious time and opportunity. This is only one simple example of how important it is for a faculty member or administrator to understand the fundamental differences between traditional students and adult learners, and as a consequence, to act accordingly.

The ongoing imperative to be sensitive to the needs of adult learners can't be emphasized enough. Perhaps Walshok (1987) captures this issue best: "The institution has a responsibility to be responsive to these publics and, even more precisely, to have a clear understanding of the specific needs and publics it is serving" (p. 150).

Andragogy Versus Pedagogy

As indicated in Chapter 2, Malcolm Knowles (1975) devoted his career to studying how humans learn and identifying those characteristics and needs that relate specifically to adult learners. His concern extended to every aspect of the learning experience. For instance, he encouraged an environment where learners felt supported rather than threatened and a climate of openness and authenticity. On a number of occasions, he suggested that when learners feel free to be open and natural—to express their thoughts without fear—they are more likely to examine new ideas and risk new behaviors. Ultimately, he saw these features as essential for a productive learning environment.

He identified the following characteristics of adult learners:

- They have a deep need to be self-directing, but they have to be helped to overcome their conditioning from previous experience, that students are dependent on teachers.

FIGURE 8.1

Classroom Distinctions Between Traditional and Adult Learners

Regarding	Pedagogy	Andragogy
Concept of learner	Dependent learner Full responsibility on instructor: what, how, when, and if material has been learned	Self-directed learner Instructors encourage and nurture
Role of learner's experience	What they bring has little worth Use of text, audiovisuals to gain experience of teacher Primary techniques include: AV presentations, lecture, assigned reading	Learner's experience is valuable Learn from experience Share experiences Primary techniques: laboratory experiments, discussion, field experiences, simulation exercises, problem-solving cases
Orientation to learning	Process of acquiring subject matter Content to be used at a much later time	Process of developing increased competence to achieve their full potential in life—ability to apply knowledge and skills more effectively tomorrow
Readiness to learn	Society determines Standard curriculum	Internally experience a need to learn Organized around life application categories

- They usually bring into any learning situation previous experience and training that provide a rich resource for helping each other learn.
- They tend to be task-centered, problem-centered, and life-centered (rather than subject-centered) in their orientation to learning.
- They are primarily intrinsically (rather than extrinsically) motivated to learn, given the right conditions and support. (pp. 129–130)

Figures 8.1 and 8.2 offer an interpretation of material presented in a paper by Leith (1998), who summarized how schools must respond to the needs of adult learners as they move from pedagogy to andragogy.

Once a program for adult learners embraces these fundamental differences between pedagogy and andragogy, the next step is to look at the conditions of learning and the corresponding principles of teaching.

Effective Strategies to Foster Learning

Chapter 6 examined the details associated with quantum learning, based in part on the work of Vella (2002). Beyond her description of how adult

Figure 8.2

The Relationship Between Conditions of Learning and Principles of Teaching for Adult Learners

Conditions of Learning	Principles of Teaching
Learners feel a need to learn	Exposes learner to new possibilities for self-fulfillment Helps with clarification of aspirations Diagnoses gap between aspirations and present level Identifies life problems experienced due to gap
Learning environment: comfortable, mutual trust, respect, mutual helpfulness, freedom of expression, acceptance of differences	Comfortable physical conditions are provided Accepts learners as persons of worth—respects their feelings and ideas Builds relationships of mutual trust and helpfulness with cooperative activities Serves as resource and colearner
Learning process is related to and makes use of experience of learners	Helps learners exploit their own experiences Gears presentations of own experiences to levels of learners Helps with applications to learning

learners demonstrate aspects of quantum learning in their everyday classroom behavior, she also presents a set of learning tasks to master. Notice how the principles presented here involve interactive dynamics between the instructor and learner, thus creating a learning-centered environment for adult learners—an element whose importance continues to be confirmed from among a growing number of sources. The 12 principles for adult learning are:

1) Effective learning will affect the learner's cognitive structures, attitudes and values and perceptions and behavioral patterns. That is, it always involves cognitive, affective and psychomotor factors.
2) People will believe more in knowledge they have discovered themselves than in knowledge presented by others.
3) Learning is more effective when it is an active rather than a passive process.
4) Acceptance of new ideas, attitudes and behavioral patterns cannot be brought about by a piecemeal approach—one's whole cognitive/affective/behavioral system (ideas/feelings/actions) has to change.
5) It takes more than information to change ideas, attitudes and behavioral patterns.
6) It takes more than firsthand experience to generate valid knowledge.
7) Behavior changes will be temporary unless the ideas and attitudes underlying them are changed.
8) Changes in perception of oneself and one's social environment are necessary before changes in ideas, attitudes and behavior will take place.
9) The more supportive, accepting and caring the social environment, the freer a person is to experiment with new behaviors, attitudes and ideas.
10) For changes in behavior patterns, attitudes and ideas to be permanent, both the person and the social environment have to change.
11) It is easier to change a person's ideas, attitudes, and behavioral patterns when he or she accepts membership in a new group. The discussion

and agreement that takes place within a group provides a personal commitment and encouragement for change that is not present when only one person is being changed.

12) A person accepts a new system of ideas, attitudes and behavioral patterns when he or she accepts membership in a new group. New groups with new role definitions and expectations for appropriate behavior are helpful in education efforts. (Johnson & Johnson, as cited in Vella, 2002, pp. 77–78)

In application, these principles require dialogue and interaction. Often, small group activities are especially helpful to maximize the impact of the principles. At the heart of this design is active learning. The concept of the "talking head"—a stationary person delivering a lecture—simply does not work (if it ever did) very effectively for adult learners. Learning in the 21st century is likely to continue to be based on the principles cited in this chapter, but even if they change (due to technology or some other unforeseen intervention), dynamic programs will remain highly flexible and responsive, as noted below.

Convenience, Flexibility, and Responsiveness

Perhaps one of the biggest challenges facing any institution seeking to expand its involvement with adult learners is its ability to make adjustments compatible with adult learner needs. Historically, most traditional colleges and universities have not been inclined to respond to change quickly or efficiently since there is seldom any motivation. As Deal (1987) indicates: "Such programs have been assured an admission pool. Once admitted, their clientele tends to stay—and to accept what it is given. To be traditional means to take a conservative stance and change very slowly, if at all" (p. 88). As a result, consumers (i.e., students) have often been forced to select among schools that basically offer a homogeneous product, with few options available to them.

In a competitive market, however, schools seeking to expand their adult enrollment have quickly learned that one of the best strategies to achieve this expansion is to be flexible, sensitive to those issues that comprise convenience for the adult learner, and quickly responsive to their needs. Despite how some faculty members may feel to the contrary, education is a business. In the adult learner arena, schools that take too long to change will lose their students to those programs that have absorbed this simple fact: Colleges and their administrators need to think and behave differently in the 21st century than ever before if they hope to attract adult learners.

"Flexible" in this context relates to those issues that increase convenience to the adult learner: schedule, location, tuition payment schedules, even procedures so long as they don't detract from the integrity of the institution. For instance, a school may offer some accelerated courses exclusively for its adult student population. As a result, it may also require special attendance policies for these same accelerated courses, since students are likely to become "at risk" more rapidly than with conventional courses. Therefore, while the institution may offer greater flexibility, it will often need to temper that flexibility with policies that protect the student while concurrently maintaining the integrity of the institution. In this regard, flexible also relates to the need for ongoing sensitivity and assessment since a successful adult program needs to constantly monitor and modify every aspect of its product.

Faculty Backgrounds and Experiences

For decades, even centuries, the ivory tower concept has implied an institution designed primarily for the privileged student. Until recently, the academy has offered significantly fewer opportunities for the remainder of the population, and even today, there are many remnants of the original impulse to be found on many campuses. According to Braskamp and Wergin (1998):

> The ivory tower seems often to be above the pain and problems of the ordinary American workforce and its daily hassles. Many educational institutions have gates, well-manicured lawns, shrubs and flowers, walls and trees to buffer the campus from the outside world. The academy does not often believe and act as though the campus is the world and the world is the campus. (pp. 62–63)

Although the post-WWII era saw colleges and universities opening their doors to a greater variety of students and at unprecedented levels of enrollment that have continued to expand, these changes have done little to influence new ways of thinking about institutions of higher learning.

This has been particularly true when it comes to the teacher-centered notion that the academy exists in much the same manner as it has for centuries. For instance, the Association of American Colleges and Universities (2002) noted:

> Ask college faculty and most will explain how they hope students will engage intellectually with the material taught. Intellectual growth comes through hard work and application to serious study. Professors anticipate students leaning what they teach, and while doing so, developing the ability to defend positions passed on knowledge rather than simple opinions. They expect students to write well and think clearly, appreciate various fields and modes of inquiry, and gain substantive knowledge in a field. The result of college education, they believe will be rational and reflective minds, open to continuous learning throughout a lifetime. From their colleges and universities, faculty members expect a collegial environment in which to teach and conduct research free from outside interference, holding to the century-old tradition of academic freedom. (p. 9)

But there is a natural tension between the faculty position and the expectations expressed by students—particularly but not exclusively, adult learners. The same report notes these expectations:

- To prepare for a good job and career advancement
- To contribute to the work environment in a dynamic economy
- To satisfy workforce needs
- To develop the capacities to reason, communicate, and respect the opinions of others
- To expand horizons and life choices
- To empower (p. 9)

In addition to the conflict of expectations between the two most prominent stakeholders in the academy, there are additional external expectations that further challenge the status quo on the 21st century campus. The Association of American Colleges and Universities (2002) has cited the following external factors that have begun to impact higher education in the 21st century enough to justify discussions regarding change.

- Changed demographics of college attendance
  - greater percentage of nontraditional students
  - more culturally diverse
  - higher proportion of high school graduates
  - many with recommended college preparatory curricula
- New enrollment patterns
  - multiple institution attendance
  - online and distance courses
- The information explosion
  - huge amount of information widely available
  - rapidly increasing
  - less review and control of quality
  - higher education no longer major repository of information
  - educational outcomes shifted from remembering facts to finding and evaluating information
- The technological revolution
  - different institutional processes
  - new jobs for graduates
  - nature of classroom changed by online learning
- A stricter regulatory environment
  - more intrusive local, state, and national regulation
  - in many states, strict standards and mandates in K–12, possibly soon in college
  - emphasis on factual recall in testing
  - greater call for accountability
  - accreditation focus on effectiveness and assessment
- New educational sites and formats
  - for-profit higher education's growth outpacing traditional colleges
  - rise of corporate university
  - more flexible learning formats and length of programs
  - much for-profit education and training largely unregulated and unaccredited (p. 6)

A quick scan confirms that the majority of these factors relate (though not always exclusively) to the adult learner. The call for change in the academy is everywhere, lending an air of inevitability even as many stakeholders continue to resist change. One cohort, the political sector, has increasingly equated economic development with level of education. In the private sector, for-profit institutions aggressively seek greater market share for themselves, which, in turn, exerts pressure on institutions to remain competitive as well. Finally, reforms and innovative practices that now reflect benchmarks as models of excellence were often first established as cutting-edge adult learner initiatives.

Faculty members who have experience with adult learners can be a particularly rich resource when it comes to issues such as faculty development for any adult program. Asking experienced faculty members who have previously taught adult learners to share their success stories is a wonderful way to develop a sense of community and good practices all at the same time.

● ● ● ● ●

One dark aspect of seeking adult learners takes place when a college or university is mainly motivated by profits derived from this population. Many faculty members and administrators who work with adult learners tend to become passionate about them. Because their stories are powerful, their aspirations so uplifting, and their determination so inspirational, adult learners often make a deep impression on many individuals who work with them. In such cases, adult learners are more likely to become a cause or premise upon which to build actions. Such is the case for Kristine who came to feel passionate about helping to meet the needs of "her" students at the school where she began working with adult learners.

Case Study: Kristine

When Kristine was hired as director for the newly formed adult program at Bennette University (BU), a small school on the outskirts of one of the nation's largest cities, with an enrollment of approximately 2,500 students, it was largely based on her success in other related ventures for the school. Although she had been working at BU for five years, she had served as coordinator for special events (commencement, matriculation ceremony, special speakers, etc.), director of the learning center, and special assistant to the president, but she had little direct experience with the academic domain of the university. As such, her skills as an entrepreneur had gained credibility but she had little experience with the special needs of adult learners. Furthermore, although she was extremely bright and talented, she lacked academic credentials since her master's degree was in organizational development.

However, Carol Williams, the president of BU, said that Kristine's credentials were exactly what she was looking for: "I want someone who can think out of the box and bring a fresh approach to this new program since it is often creativity and fresh thinking that have defined some of the very best adult programs." What Carol didn't say, though Kristine was already fully aware of the underlying message, was that BU was hoping to secure and build its shaky financial status based on an anticipated substantial enrollment of adult learners. And when Kristine protested about her lack of formal background, Dr. Williams responded, "You are a quick study, we will give you a window of time to grow and develop. I know you will draw heavily from your own experiences as an adult learner when you completed your own degree, and we will enable you to experience some of the most notable adult programs, first hand." There were, however, other assurances that Kristine later wished she had received at this time but in her enthusiasm, she made some unfounded assumptions.

Kristine worked tirelessly during the six-month period prior to the introduction of the first adult courses at BU. She visited three campuses and examined every aspect of their programs, from curriculum to infrastructure and publications. Ultimately, Kristine felt she had a clear picture of what was required to produce a successful quality adult program. Under her leadership, BUCAS—the BU Center for Adult Students—was created. She had formed a faculty advisory council to ensure the program had the support of all faculty members. They were given extensive curricular control and, whenever possible, she tried to honor their requests or respond with alternatives she had absorbed from reading the many books written by the early trailblazers in this field. In drawing from her own background, she created a student-centered program that would always be a first priority. By the time the program actually began, Kristine had added two final elements that brought an extraordinary level of support to adult learners: a day-care program available for the children of evening and weekend students, and three dorm rooms set aside for weekend students who might otherwise have to travel impossible distances. She also spent countless hours meeting with every possible constituency in order to understand their needs, minimize problems, and make certain everyone was on the same page. However, shortly after the program began, many of her high hopes began to fade.

Like many other adult programs, the BUCAS initiative was proposed by a president seeking an easy fiscal solution to the decline in income BU had been experiencing over the past five years. President Williams put her faith in Kristine because she was bright, energetic, and creative. However, BU's financial situation had become so weak that there was no margin for error or flexibility. In short order, Kristine realized that BU was unable to support the sort of initiatives that good start-up programs require—things that always come down to time and money. Indeed, the entire BUCAS program was expected to run on the barest of budgets and thinnest of margins. What she quickly learned was that BU had expected Kristine's program to turn an immediate profit.

Whenever Kristine went to Dr. Williams to argue that "you have to spend money to make it," she only got a stony response about a lack of funds available to underwrite her program. Although Kristine loved working with the BUCAS program, she continued to feel frustrated and betrayed. Eventually, although the program continued to struggle, any success associated with the BUCAS initiative was easily attributed to Kristine's commitment to service and quality as her efforts began to draw attention from other schools.

Nonetheless, she was disappointed when she finally went to Dr. Williams to explain the offer she had received from a competitor in the same region: "She didn't even try to keep me. It was obvious that all she was thinking about was saving money by getting a less expensive replacement now that the program was established." Although the new offer was extremely generous, Kristine had held out the hope that BU would appreciate all her hard work and want to somehow reward her with recognition for her efforts.

Kristine is now directing an adult program that is solid and reputable. Although she doesn't have a lavish budget, it supports the new initiatives she has introduced and has given her time to prove the worthiness of her new projects. The program has a renewed commitment to service and quality that has gradually paid a dividend. In addition to the enrollment increasing, Kristine is working in a positive, healthy culture that supports her vision and treats her with respect. The best part is Kristine is finally getting what she had hoped to achieve in the first place: fulfillment and a deep sense of accomplishment.

● ● ● ● ●

Conclusion

Some factors unique to the 21st century are likely to influence today's adult learner population in ways that might have seemed inconceivable until recently. For instance, the graying of America in general is only beginning to affect marketing strategies. However, there is already ample evidence that a trend is building where, for the first time in memory, attention is shifting from the youth market to recognition of both the buying power and influence of the so-called Boomer generation. Bundle this trend with the inevitable expansion of adult enrollment at colleges and universities and the result is a powerful demographic comprised of discriminating consumers that can't simply be taken for granted.

Many schools, however, are likely to view this population as a commodity or merely a source of income rather than as a distinctive population worthy of special effort or consideration. But given the rise in competition for the adult student market, the competitive edge is often likely to be determined by such simple factors as responsiveness to need, flexibility of programs, quality of product or reputation, or other highly subjective factors that may rely heavily on the perceptions of the target audience.

In the final analysis, there probably isn't a great deal of difference between the product of one school and another. The three factors that influence adult learners above all others are convenience, time, and money. When competing programs don't offer any significant advantage in any of these crucial areas, students will seek other reasons to help them in their selection.

A perfect example of this phenomenon is represented by the two primary choices adult learners faced in one region where I worked. On the one hand, students could select a major school that had multiple satellite campuses throughout the nation with an adult program based exclusively on students selecting a specific evening with an expectation that, for the next two or more years, all of their courses would be offered at that time.

The convenience for these students was that they didn't have to worry about registration for their next class, nor worry about whether their class might be filled or canceled. Furthermore, they also didn't need to worry about adjusting any part of their schedule since it would remain the same for the entire duration of their program. In fact, even their classroom might not change from one class to the next, so there was a built-in factor of consistency and continuity in this design that appealed to many adult learners.

In contrast, our program also was designed exclusively for adult learners but we never really thought of ourselves in competition with this other program since we saw the needs of our students as quite different and distinctive. We had determined that the reasons our students preferred our program actually reflected two primary considerations: flexibility and quality. Our program offered the adult learner a wide range of scheduling options, so that the students could pick when they wanted their courses, the sequence of their courses, and who would teach their courses. We confirmed that these options gave our students what they said they wanted. We also recognized that not all adult students were seeking the same thing, which is why we didn't see ourselves in competition with the other program. They were simply responding to the needs of another group of adult learners.

Since our tuitions were similar and the time required to complete the degree was equivalent, each of our programs had identified special needs of our adult learners and responded appropriately. Ultimately, understanding these needs helped us articulate our unique market niche and identify a realistic expectation for our enrollment. But perhaps the greatest benefit we accrued from this understanding came in the form of retention. We were able to maintain extremely high retention among our students as a result of our ongoing efforts to assess their needs and to respond accordingly.

We may have taken a page from the other school in this regard. That is, we focused our strategy on the local population of adult learners because that was the audience we hoped to attract. The other school had gained much of its success by the same practice at the national level. Although I can't attest to its success regarding retention, its national enrollment continues to grow and its emphasis on responding to the needs of its students has begun to attract serious attention.

References

Association of American Colleges and Universities. (2002). *Greater expectations: A new vision for learning as a nation goes to college.* Washington, DC: Author.

Braskamp, L. A., & Wergin, J. F. (1998). Forming new social partnerships. In W. G. Tierney (Ed.), *The responsive university: Restructuring for high performance* (pp. 62–91). Baltimore, MD: The Johns Hopkins University Press.

Brendler, B., & Vonk, S. (2002, May). Creating a customer-centric culture through organizational assessment. Retrieved May 10, 2002, from http:/www.crmguru.com/features/2002b/0509bb.html

Chaffee, E. E. (1998). Listening to the people we serve. In W. G. Tierney (Ed.), *The responsive university: Restructuring for high performance* (pp. 13–37). Baltimore, MD: The Johns Hopkins University Press.

Deal, T. E. (1987). Building an effective organizational culture: How to be community-oriented in a traditional institution. In R. G. Simerly (Ed.), *Strategic planning and leadership in continuing education* (pp. 87–102), San Francisco, CA: Jossey-Bass.

Knowles, M. S. (1975). *Self-directed learning: A guide for learners and teachers.* New York, NY: Cambridge Books.

Leith, K. P. (1998, May). *Adult learning styles and critical thinking in psychology 100/101.* Paper presented at the meeting of the American Psychological Society Convention, Washington, DC.

Schmidt, J. W. (1987). The leader's role in strategic planning. In R. G. Simerly (Ed.), *Strategic planning and leadership in continuing education* (pp. 31–50). San Francisco, CA: Jossey-Bass.

Vella, J. (2002, Spring). Quantum learning: Teaching as dialogue. *New Directions for Adult and Continuing Education, 93,* 73–83.

Walshok, M. L. (1987). Developing a strategic marketing plan. In R. G Simerly (Ed.), *Strategic planning and leadership in continuing education* (pp. 149–167). San Francisco, CA: Jossey-Bass.

9

Stepping Into the Void

OVERVIEW

Although they may not always show it, a significant number of adult students are terrified to return to or attend college as adult learners. This chapter examines the critical processes of readiness and syntheses most adult learners encounter in their passage from seeking admission to experiencing their first few classes and the critical role instructors may play in supporting this transition.

Even though this situation extends beyond the limits of how an institution may overtly respond, adult learners still expect their instructors to be interested in them and their unique needs and to understand the obstacles they encounter in their pursuit of higher education. In short, adult learners are likely to contend that faculty members treat them like second-class students when they fail to demonstrate understanding and sensitivity to the special problems they face and the sense of trauma they likely overcame just to begin their educational journey.

INTRODUCTION

While the previous chapter examined institutional responses to the needs of adult learners, this chapter focuses on a more generalized form of response that depends on the sensitivity of the individual faculty member. This practice is consistent with the findings of Bers and Smith (as cited in Watson, 2001) who claimed that "a supportive, challenging instructor was instrumental in adult student success" (p. 25).

While a faculty member's attitude, sensitivity, and demeanor regarding adult learners is critical to their success, these characteristics are also likely to strongly influence the success of the instructor as well. In other words, adult learners are more likely to respond positively to a classroom environment where they are valued, understood, and appreciated rather than a hostile or adversarial situation. These characteristics are consistent with the construction of learning communities. As Shapiro and Levine (1999) suggest, "Although there is less empirical research available on the impact of learning communities on faculty, those who teach in learning communities report changed attitudes and approaches toward pedagogy and stronger interactions with students and colleagues" (p. 192).

Indeed, given the greater vulnerability of many adult learners (in part attributed to the reduced academic fluency associated with having been away from formal learning for many years), they are often jeopardized by faculty members who have unrealistic expectations (i.e., using the same pedagogical approach and criteria they do for traditional students) or antagonistic attitudes. The give and take nature of this relationship is often overlooked when it comes to institutional responses to adult learners but when carefully considered, it can provide a win/win solution for all constituents.

Many professors, and even institutions, are mistaken in their belief that all students should be treated the same or that they have the same needs and backgrounds. Perhaps they should think more like farmers, who understand that different crops have different needs that will affect their growth and productivity. For instance, while some crops may require full sunlight and lots of water, others will flourish best under significantly different circumstances. Likewise, various soil conditions and fertilizer requirements are likely to influence the productivity of the harvest for each crop differently. Adult learners require more attention and certainly more understanding than their younger classmates. That is not to say, however, that they are so delicate they will wither away if they don't receive the proper attention. But if the objective is to maximize their productivity, the instructor (as farmer) will want to provide an environment that is as conducive to learning for adult learners as possible and be mindful that this will probably require a different approach than he or she uses in a classroom filled with traditional-aged students.

Consequently, one developmental step that institutions may use to address this situation is to increase the awareness and consciousness of the faculty assigned to adult learners. Although there is a growing body of literature to support and supplement this topic, administrators handing out articles seldom accomplish the level of intervention required to change behaviors and expectations. Therefore, faculty development sessions focusing specifically on the needs and support sought by adult learners typically prove to be the most effective response to this problem. Furthermore, while they are participating in faculty development activities, faculty members also function in much the same manner as adult learners so they have an opportunity to gain insights from a student perspective.

What they won't encounter in this experience, however, are the initial impulses that often drive the adult learner into the classroom in the first place. Although it is impossible to capture each individual's story in this regard, a broad brush helps provide some insights and background concerning the majority of adult learners.

INTRODUCING: REAL COURAGE

Because adults have a greater array of experiences to draw upon, and because most have been socialized to hide or, at least, suppress any display of their anxiety or fear, it may not be readily noticeable for the instructor. But fear is what adults are most likely to self-describe, especially when they are beginning their studies. Students are likely to describe their emotional reaction as strong (especially at the beginning of each new course), and while it may not be readily observable, these feelings certainly exist for the vast majority of adult learners. In fact, many faculty members would be amazed to discover the level of extreme discomfort or anxiety the students may be experiencing in their classroom. Of course, for the students to even discuss this topic, there needs to be a level of trust and openness that some faculty members don't cultivate or earn. Nonetheless, and this can't be emphasized enough, many adult learners report profound levels of fear and apprehension when it comes to new classes, new learning experiences, and the college experience in general.

Fear is a very real manifestation of the decision process for the adult learner. It is simply part of the human condition to be less than enthusiastic about change under the best of circumstances. For meaningful change to take place, compelling reasons are almost a prerequisite. For adults actively seeking college-level learning after a number of years' absence, compounded for many by their less-than-satisfactory previous experiences with school, they may be facing the most daunting decision of their life.

To better understand the degree of their discomfort, picture Indiana Jones in the movie *Indiana Jones and The Last Crusade* where he is expected to step into the bottomless void in his pursuit of the sacred chalice that will save his father's life—a leap of faith if there ever was one. Many adult learners report having the same sensation as they begin their entry or reentry into college-level learning—they are as terrified as they are compelled to take that step.

While it requires different periods of adjustment for various adult learners, the intense feelings many students experience is near phobic. It is because these students are willing to overcome such fears and anxieties that they should be viewed as courageous. Indeed, probably even more adults would be enrolled in college-level courses if they felt reassured that their efforts would be met with compassion, support, and understanding (not to be confused with dilution, reduction of standards and expectations, or lack of rigor).

It is difficult to convey the emotional roller coaster most adult students experience each time they consider matriculating. In part, of course, this can be attributed to facing the unknown—a challenging task for anyone. But it is usually the emotional baggage that is frequently revealed by the prospective adult student (even as early as first discussions with admission counselors) that helps to explain the full depth of feelings most adults bring with them. In many instances, gut-wrenching fear or other self-esteem issues comprise gigantic obstacles for adult learners. Therefore, it's no surprise that one of the words frequently used by experienced faculty and administrators to describe adult learners is "courageous."

The Adult Learner's Rule of Conservation

Piaget, the famous learning psychologist, created an experiment defining "conservation" for youngsters to demonstrate their developmental learning level. The experiment utilizes a tall, cylindrical water jar and a flat object such as a pie plate, where water from one is transferred to the other in front of the subject (typically, a youngster less than nine years of age). Piaget observed that the ability to understand the concept that the volume of water is the same, regardless of the size or shape of the container, is only achieved at a specified level of readiness (usually, somewhere around the ninth year). Prior to that time of readiness, the subject will perceive one of the containers as having more water than the other. But once the subject is able to grasp this concept, he or she has also achieved an internal level of understanding that applies to many other more sophisticated applications as well.

Although adult learners have no comparable quantifiable learning level development, many do experience the concept of "readiness" that functions in much the same way. That is, they reach a point in their lives where the notion of pursuing a degree or certificate becomes so compelling that they feel forced to act. In many cases, adults report spending an extended period (sometimes years) thinking casually or informally about taking college-level courses. They may even articulate their thoughts, but they aren't yet ready to act on those thoughts. However, similar to the example regarding the law of conservation, when adults do achieve a level of readiness, their interest in pursuing college-level studies sharply increases. In most instances, this is usually accomplished internally through reflection and introspection, though as noted in previous chapters, external factors sometimes contribute as well.

The Epiphany

For many adults, there is a moment—often isolated and galvanized in their memory—when the necessity to pursue college-level learning comes into sharp focus. Cartoonists capture this by drawing a lightbulb over a subject's head to symbolize the "Eureka!" moment. A large segment of adult learners say they experience such an epiphany. But such a moment doesn't just happen in a vacuum. For adult learners, there is often an extended period of time that involves reflection, calculation, and information seeking. In short, the adult learner typically experiences a form of gestation prior to reaching that final point of decision. This situation reflects what Knowles (1990) refers to when he says, "A prerequisite for effective learning to take place is the establishment of a climate that is conducive to learning" (p. 126).

When adults ultimately do reach this stage, they tend to want to get started as quickly as possible. Even though it might have taken them years to process the information and reach the point where they can envision themselves as college students, once they get to that plateau, they typically express a sense of impatience to begin, as well as to achieve closure. The situation might be analogous to diving from a great height. If the diver has a strong incentive, even though he or she may be very fearful, an onlooker can almost see that moment when the individual decides to take action. Even though they understand they are leaping into the void, they are committed to making the effort rather than holding back.

The Internal Challenge

Most adult students come with a king-sized supply of self-doubt so they are likely to seek confirmation and reassurance concerning their decision. Because they draw from life experiences, most adults have achieved a healthy level of skepticism by the time they are prepared to enter an institution of higher learning. Most adult learners "come from Missouri" (the "show me" state) so that even though they may have made the decision to go to college and fully understand the wisdom of their decision—and perhaps even have confidence about the conclusions they have drawn during the process—their fear of the unknown is profound. Even when they are highly successful, adults are likely to express genuine and sincere reservations about their capacity to succeed as college students.

Although this attitude is probably more realistic than that displayed by their younger classmates, who are more likely to see themselves as invincible or indifferent, adult learners tend to understand that they are at a junction where their options are reduced, they will probably have to face significant sacrifice, and there is little margin for error. Therefore, they are likely to see themselves as more vulnerable. They are often highly sensitized to the classroom environment and the instructor's demeanor toward them, especially since they often believe they have something to prove. Adult learners are more likely to seek affirmation through good grades and other overt signs of success on the campus than traditional students are. Conversely, they are often less inclined to take their success for granted.

The tension between their vulnerability and pursuit of success frequently does create a sense of internal struggle that adds to their overall stress. The dilemma adult learners are likely to face, therefore, often tends to be internal in nature, reinforced by their sense of urgency, their reservations emanating from self-esteem and self-confidence issues, their compulsion to succeed, and the inevitable transformation associated with learning new concepts and encountering new ideas. It is no wonder, then, that higher education for this population tends to leave such a dramatic, life-altering impression.

FACULTY RESPONSES TO THESE ISSUES

In stark contrast to circumstances cited in the previous chapter, where the institutional response to the adult learner is the pivotal factor, there are many issues that can only be addressed in the classroom by the individual professor. Various responses have been identified in this regard. Two important citations offer alternative, though somewhat overlapping, criteria any instructor may wish to consider when working predominantly with adult learners. While the first study (Billington, 1996) looks at the classroom as an environment where the professor actively and intentionally seeks to control aspects of the ambience, the second (Chickering & Gamson, 1987) relates to the evaluation of the teacher, based on many years of higher education research.

Billington (1996) investigated which factors in adult learning environments best facilitate adult growth and development. She determined that adult students grew significantly only in one type of learning environment. Note how the characteristics she identified relate to the role of the instructor. In fact, his or her skills are critical in determining success for the learner. The characteristics include:

1) An environment where students feel safe and supported, where individual needs and uniqueness are honored, where abilities and life achievements are acknowledged and respected.

2) An environment that fosters intellectual freedom and encourages experimentation and creativity.

3) An environment where faculty treats adult students as peers—accepted and respected as intelligent, experienced adults whose opinions are listened to, honored, appreciated. Such faculty members often comment that they learn as much from their students as the students learn from them.

4) Self-directed learning, where students take responsibility for their own learning. They work with faculty to design individual learning programs which address what each person needs and wants to learn in order to function optimally in their profession.

5) Pacing, or intellectual challenge. Optimal pacing is challenging people just beyond their present level of ability. If challenged too far beyond, people give up. If challenged too little, they become bored and

learn little. Pacing can be compared to playing tennis with a slightly better player; your game tends to improve. But if the other player is far better and it's impossible to return a ball, you give up, overwhelmed. If the other player is less experienced and can return none of your balls, you learn little. Those adults who reported experiencing high levels of intellectual stimulation—to the point of feeling discomfort—grew more.

6) Active involvement in learning, as opposed to passively listening to lectures. Where students and instructors interact and dialogue, where students try out new ideas in the workplace, where exercises and experiences are used to bolster facts and theory, adults grow more.

7) Regular feedback mechanisms for students to tell faculty what works best for them and what they want and need to learn—and faculty who hear and make changes based on student input. (Billington, 1996, p. 2)

Billington (1996) also found that:

> In learning programs where students feel unsafe and threatened, where they are viewed as underlings, life achievements not honored, those students tend to regress developmentally, especially in self-esteem and self-confidence. In programs where students are required to take identical lockstep courses, whether relevant to professional goals or not, and where they are often expected to spend several years working on a dissertation that is part of a professor's research project instead of on a topic of their choice, they grow less. In other words, students grow more in student-centered as opposed to faculty-centered programs. (p. 2)

Chickering and Gamson (1987) published "Seven Principles for Good Practice in Undergraduate Education" in what has become a classic strategy for evaluating teaching for adult learners. The principles are articulated below.

1) Good practice encourages student-faculty contact.

2) Good practice encourages cooperation among students.

3) Good practice encourages active learning.

4) Good practice gives prompt feedback.

5) Good practice emphasizes time on task.

6) Good practice communicates high expectations.

7) Good practice respects diverse talents and ways of learning. (p. 3)

Note how both sets are learner-centered and how some of the characteristics and principles tend to reinforce one another. Although an instructor wouldn't have to utilize both sets in order to be successful in a classroom of adult learners, they are presented in the hope that at least one would be consciously implemented. This is critical since faculty response is more likely to influence adult learners than any other single institutional response.

"Transformation" Classes

One institutional response that may help build a bridge between learners and faculty and has proven to be particularly helpful in assisting adults when they are ready to begin their collegiate experience is the use of introductory "transformation" classes. These courses tend to serve as a link between the world the adult knows and the academy he or she is about to enter (Bash, Lighty, & Tebrock, 1999). Such courses (typically the adult equivalent of College 101 for incoming freshmen) provide the following benefits for the adult learner.

- Introduce and orient new students to the specific institution and what makes it distinctive for adult learners
- Help the students make adjustments to college-level work while preparing them for some of the potential problems they are likely to encounter as adult learners
- Prepare the students for the responsibilities they are about to assume and understand what faculty members typically seek in good students
- Acquaint the student's family or significant others with some of the notable challenges they are likely to encounter even as they learn to provide a support system for the adult learner

- Familiarize the students with the various opportunities they are likely to encounter, help them to gain a holistic understanding of how the school operates along with its expectations
- Assist students to develop their skills with tools and strategies (Bash, Lighty, & Tebrock, 1999, pp. 1–2)

Perhaps the greatest advantages derived from such courses relate to the foundation of skills and strategies provided as a resource and means to assist the student to gain confidence in himself or herself (see Billington, 1996, as noted above). Adult learners consistently report that such a course, designed to explicitly respond to the needs of adult learners and carefully created to give adult learners a sense of worth by reinforcing the common experiences shared by their classmates, provides the students with a concrete frame of reference to help support further learning endeavors.

Due perhaps to the disproportionate number of adult learners who are women, and the fact that more women tend to be abused in our society, an unfortunate number of adult learners come into the classroom under a less than pleasant—even dark—set of circumstances. Billie is one such case. A 47-year-old who has devoted her life to raising her family and providing a comfortable home for her husband, she has a deer-in-the-headlights look about her that makes her pain all too obvious when she comes for her admissions interview. When her husband suddenly declared that he was leaving her and her teenaged children two months ago, she was shocked. However, when she realized that she had no marketable skills and that her husband was basically abandoning her, she finally realized how isolated and vulnerable she really was. She has begun reassembling her life, but her fear and vulnerability live barely below the surface of her being so that, when you are around her, you are certain she will break into tears at any moment.

The good news for Billie is that this shocking set of events has forced her to do a lot of in-depth thinking about herself and to do so in a very brief amount of time. She may not feel very good about herself and she certainly isn't confident about her ability to actually sustain herself as a college student. But once she decided that going to college was the best solution to protect her from ever being this vulnerable again, she has be-

come determined to do the very best she can so that if she somehow fails, it won't be because she didn't try.

Case Study: Billie's Blues

The very first course Billie took at Fairview College was "Principles of Adult Learning" that all adult students are required to complete before they can take any other courses. The first night of class took place on a Friday evening, and even though pizza was provided for all the students, Billie wasn't sure she would ever be able to eat again. Despite how calm and reassuring the instructor seemed to be, by the time the class was assembled and ready to begin, Billie was so nervous that she had actually begun to break out in hives.

Since the class had a preclass assignment, Billie already knew that part of the first evening would be devoted to each student sharing his or her story to explain how they had ended up as an entering student at Fairview. The very idea of speaking in front of the other 22 students in this class was already making Billie nauseous. But when her instructor, Dr. Leyte, suggested that each student was going to be asked to share someone else's story after the first round was complete (in order to help students get to know one another but also improve their listening and note-taking skills), Billie was certain she would faint before the evening was over.

And then, something almost magical began to happen. Fortunately, the first person called on to relate his story to the class was on the other side of the room. (If Dr. Leyte had called on her first, she envisioned herself running and screaming out of the classroom.) Billie noted that even before the first student was asked to begin, Dr. Leyte used his own story to serve as a model for the students. His story was full of hard work and sacrifices, and reminded all of the students that even though he was now a professor, he had once been an adult learner just like them. By the time the third student was telling her story, Billie's heart was beginning to pound less and she was beginning to understand that while everyone in the room faced his or her own unique set of challenges and that each of them had some hardships they had been forced to overcome prior to enrolling in this course, they all shared much in common.

According to her notes, as she reviewed the class later that evening, one student had lost a husband to cancer and three students were being "downsized." They were facing serious challenges in getting new jobs since they lacked degrees, even if they did have extensive knowledge and experience. Almost one-third of the class was comprised of students whose workplace expectations were now based on explicit criteria that included a degree. Some had been told that if they ever hoped to receive another promotion, it would only happen with a degree.

By the time it was Billie's turn, she was already beginning to feel a certain trust and bond with her classmates, though she still felt terrified beyond belief. She decided that the watered-down "safe" story she had been rehearsing probably wouldn't really ring true in this group and so she went for uncluttered honesty instead: "Hello, my name is Billie. I am 47 years old and I am more frightened than I have ever been in my life. In fact, I am breaking out in hives! I am starting out as a college student with no former experience, either as a student or in the job market. I have devoted my life to making a comfortable home for my family and husband. I am here tonight because my husband has left me to live with a younger woman. I have two teenagers who have been incredibly supportive. When I told them about my decision to enroll in college, they offered to help in any way possible. For instance, on the evenings when I have class, they will prepare dinner for me and they have also agreed to take on one additional chore. My daughter will do laundry every week (which I hate anyway) and my son has indicated that he will vacuum every week. If anything, this situation has strengthened the bond I have with my children. They tell me they have faith and confidence in me and even though my life feels like it has exploded in some ways and is falling apart in others, I have never felt more fortunate."

As Billie tells her story, tears stream down her cheeks, perhaps in fear or perhaps in grief, she isn't sure. But she also notes that in this room, she feels a level of support and understanding unlike anything she has encountered before. It is beyond anything she ever expected in a classroom. She is already beginning to form some very positive impressions about Fairview if this is how they treat their adult learners. When she is done, Dr. Leyte gently thanks her before telling a brief story about a previous student who had a similar background who went on to graduate with honors. Billie doesn't even care whether the story is true. She is overwhelmingly reassured that she is understood and still respected rather than treated like the loser her husband had described and she was beginning to feel she might be. For the first time in a long time, she also believes things may actually work out.

At the break later, Billie finds that she no longer feels isolated or alone. In fact, she discovers that she has already begun to make friends with three of her classmates. At the end of class that evening, Dr. Leyte gives the class a huge stack of handouts and materials as an assignment to be read and discussed for the next class. But just as the work begins to look overwhelming to Billie, he also shows the students how to use their time wisely and helps them understand which of the pieces are more important than others. With Dr. Leyte's sensitive prodding and support, Billie begins to even impress herself later that evening at how much she is able to accomplish. She now understands what he meant when he told the class, "For those of you who are willing to do the work, you will amaze yourself at your progress. I intend to push you, but if you're organized and apply yourself, you will achieve more than you may think possible."

By the end of the course, everyone agrees that they have done an incredible amount of work. But they also discover many aspects about themselves that help give them confidence concerning their future classes. For instance, Billie has gotten in touch with her creative side for part of her final project. When Dr. Leyte asks her to share her work with her classmates so they can all see how well she has done, she is almost as red in the face as she was on the first evening, but now she is also flushed with a sense of success and relief.

Billie knows she has a huge amount of work in front of her. Dr. Leyte has warned her that some of this work will be incredibly difficult so that she may even be tempted to quit. But her resolve is stronger than ever, bolstered by a sense of confidence and self-esteem she would not have believed possible at the beginning of the course. In Billie's mind there is only one acceptable outcome: Every day for the remainder of the time until her dream becomes her reality, Billie pictures herself walking across the stage after her name is called and receiving her diploma. When that day actually happens, Billie only confirms again something she has learned in that very first course—she can do anything she sets her mind to accomplish!

● ● ● ● ●

As adult learners continue to comprise an increasing portion of the total enrollment in higher education, market pressures are likely to influence some schools to add new programs for them, based primarily on their financial income potential. Some schools that are already "at risk" may take a narrow view of adult learners as a solution to their financial problems so that they lose sight of other related issues. This situation can be exacerbated by the decision to outsource the adult program to external sources. But schools and their leaders who seek adult learners primarily based on bottom line considerations may find themselves facing problems relating to infrastructure, faculty, curriculum, and identity that they may never have anticipated in the first place. Under such circumstances, these schools may be forced to either reconsider or eliminate their adult program or agreement with external companies. Unfortunately, Bill Gardner, President of Iconic Diminutive College, has learned these lessons the hard way. As a result, his bid to have the adult program accredited and offered at various satellite locations has been denied by his regional accrediting body. As a result, he is now singing his own special version of the blues.

Case Study: Bill's Blues

As president of Iconic Diminutive College (IDC), Bill Gardner is a little pepper pot of activity and ideas. When he became IDC's tenth president he did so with the full knowledge that the school had a host of intimidating challenges. At the root of all those challenges was a fiscal situation that didn't provide for any error and very little movement relating to new initiatives and mission. By declaring exigency and calling upon all stakeholders to make sacrifices, he had been able to buy some time. However, the progress was hard fought and Bill was concerned that the resources he had to call on simply weren't enough to breathe new life into the tiny school that had managed to serve its wonderful students by such a dedicated staff for many decades. But Bill saw himself as a change agent and idea man who just needed the right solutions to turn the situation around, once and for all.

It was under these circumstances that Bill was contacted by the Adult Learner Fast Track (ALFT) group with an impressive proposal. ALFT was willing to bring in their prepackaged curriculum, pay the faculty for developmental sessions, provide money for advertising, and even contribute some computers to IDC. All they wanted in return was a specified percentage of the income. Furthermore, ALFT explained that IDC would "own" the program so that there would not be any overt references to ALFT. As far as the public would be concerned, this would simply be a new IDC initiative. In addition, IDC would have to seek new accreditation since the adult programs would ultimately be offered off-campus. Although the margin that ALFT would receive in this agreement seemed rather steep, Debbie Sweeney, the vice president from ALFT, pointed out that they were taking all the risks. So any profit IDC would receive would be at no risk to them and would amount to something more than if they didn't even try. In the meantime, she encouraged Bill to bring a team of faculty and administrators to other ALFT-affiliated schools to observe their programs and see how much money they were making.

Both the ALFT schools the IDC team visited did, in fact, seem to be showing an impressive profit on the balance sheet. However, faculty members from the team were quick to point out that the vast majority of the instructors were adjuncts, a practice the IDC faculty had emphatically eschewed since they prided themselves in the amount of attention they paid to their students. Furthermore, the faculty members also expressed serious reservations about the rigor of the coursework. As one faculty member said, "There doesn't appear to be much substance to challenge the learners. We saw ALFT students doing 'upper level' work that I would have described as basic. If our IDC students turned in material like that, we would have declared it unsatisfactory."

On the other hand, the administrative members of the team were impressed. The ALFT programs seemed to be well organized and to run smoothly. Everyone (including faculty members) was envious of the advertising budget the ALFT programs enjoyed since IDC had been reduced to a minimal amount of advertising for their own school. As one faculty member put it, "At least IDC might be able to gain some attention through this program so we aren't merely 'the best kept secret east of the Mississippi' any more."

Although there had been little discussion of a timeline up to this point, shortly after the team came back from its second visit, Bill received a call from Debbie. "Bill, we've done some research for you. We've been assured that your regional accrediting body will let you move ahead for up to two years as a pilot if we can get the proper paperwork together in the next four months. At the same time, there are three other schools that are in much the same position and we are only prepared to partner with one of you at this time."

In fact, Bill had been working over the numbers and, based on some figures derived from other ALFT schools, he believed IDC could generate a million dollar profit in the first year. After conferring with his senior staff, he and his academic dean called the seven department chairs together to share their vision and proposal. As Bill told them in early April, "I know you may have some reservations about ALFT programs, but they are willing to work with you to satisfy any concerns. If we take advantage of this opportunity and our projections become a reality, you will be the direct beneficiaries of the additional income." Later, the chairs would claim that they didn't really feel like they had any option other than to accept ALFT as a partner.

For the remainder of the school year and well into the summer, the campus was extremely busy. While most of the faculty members appreciated the extra money they received from ALFT to work on parts of the special curriculum (IDC didn't offer summer courses), many of them resented the use of time that they would have otherwise dedicated to research. Furthermore, a subtle, tacit undercurrent began to emerge among the faculty during this time. Finally, an English professor articulated what many of her colleagues had been thinking. "I'm looking forward to finally having some money to support our regular students, but none of this seems like it is really a part of the IDC culture and I'm not going to do anything special in order to make it succeed." Interestingly, since it had already been agreed that the new program was going to rely on adjunct faculty and weekend classes (the satellite sites were expected to be in place by the time they received full accreditation) the administration was largely unaware of this undercurrent.

Throughout the summer, ALFT placed a number of ads on radio, billboards, and in the newspaper. The faculty, who had begrudgingly cobbled a curriculum together according to ALFT guidelines, were pleased to see the new attention IDC was receiving, but otherwise, they were taking a wait and see attitude. At the beginning of the fall term, despite the hard work of many, the enrollment figures reflected only the minimum enrollment IDC and ALFT had agreed upon in advance. In addition, although IDC had managed to start the program according to the agreed upon timeline, faculty members noted a growing number of concerns regarding infrastructure, support, admission's policies, and other issues outside the curriculum. Among themselves, however, they agreed that the best strategy was to keep their distance, not buy in, but at least think about how their departments might use the extra money they envisioned.

The accrediting body sent a two-person team at the beginning of the second year. By now, the program was beginning to have its own identity. Unfortunately, the original enrollment in the first cohort had now been reduced to seven students—below the acceptable minimum. At this point, neither ALFT nor IDC were making any money from the first cohort but both agreed that, for the program to move ahead, they had to sustain this smaller class. In the meantime, modest gains were made regarding the enrollment of each cohort. By the time the fourth cohort was ready to begin, the numbers were higher than ever before, though still below anticipated projections. The entire campus viewed the accrediting team's visit with anticipation since the faculty reasoned that once the program was accepted, it would move off campus (where it might even flourish) and generate even more money for the main campus. Likewise, the administration, who had been struggling with deferred maintenance issues for some time, continued to hope that this would be the antidote they had been searching for as well.

During the visit, however, things began to unravel. Although the team was concerned from the beginning about the lack of faculty investment, they had encountered other schools that had made extensive use of adjunct faculty without serious damage to the curriculum. However, in the course of a meeting between one of the evaluators and faculty members, the evaluator was dismayed to hear the answer to what he thought was an innocent question: "What happens when an adult student in your ALFT program decides to become a full-time student at IDC?" It was the English professor, who had become an unofficial spokesperson, who answered: "We could not, in good faith, accept any of the credits from the ALFT program toward degree completion at IDC." When most of the other faculty members in attendance murmured and nodded their agreement, the evaluator knew that there could only be one logical consequence of the team's visit.

Later, when the team mentioned the faculty response to Bill and his academic dean, neither person indicated much surprise. In fact, Bill's answer was, "Well, maybe we can establish articulation agreements with other schools in the area if our ALFT students feel like they need to continue their studies elsewhere."

Today, IDC is still struggling to survive. At times, the margin to stay open is razor thin. But the students who attend love the school and the special attention they receive from the dedicated faculty and staff. IDC has agreed that they will focus on what they do best and that will be their niche, as narrowly defined as possible. Bill moved on to another position the year after the report from the accrediting body was submitted to IDC. ALFT is still seeking at-risk schools to host their programs and share in their profits.

●●●●●

Conclusion

Colleges and universities that are serious about providing quality education for their adult learners must devote a significant portion of their energy and resources toward faculty development. Otherwise, they are like a high-powered automobile that requires high-octane gasoline in order to run smoothly and efficiently. If the owner decides to use a lower grade of gasoline, the car will still function but eventually, the weaker gasoline will damage the engine and it may even break down.

Many trailblazers in the field of adult education have noted variations on the same theme on how these students should be regarded and treated. Successful instructors understand the ongoing pressures that adult learners face with their hectic schedules and extensive responsibilities along with the incredible emotional challenges they must overcome just to begin and then sustain their studies.

While institutions can provide special schedules, accelerated formats, cohort programs, and other issues that relate to infrastructure, one critical factor that is beyond most institutional consideration is the role of the individual instructor. As the dean of a division devoted exclusively to adult learners, the overwhelming number of complaints and concerns I encounter from my students relate to two primary faculty profiles: 1) those who don't understand the differences between adult learners and traditional students and therefore treat them all the same, and 2) those who may even understand the differences but aren't willing to invest the extra amount of effort required to respond to them. Of the two, most complaints are directed at the first group while the second are a distinct minority. Nonetheless, intervention in the guise of faculty development is clearly the easiest activity to assure that these complaints and concerns are minimized.

References

Bash, L., Lighty, K., & Tebrock, D. (1999). Utilizing a "transformation" course to assist returning adult learners. *Proceedings of Alliance/ACE Conference, 19,* 1–5.

Billington, D. D. (1996, May/June). Seven characteristics of highly effective adult learning programs. *New Horizons Electronic Journal.* Retrieved May 20, 2002, from http://www.newhorizons.org/article_billington1.html

Chickering, A., & Gamson, Z. (1987). Seven principles of good practice in undergraduate education. *AAHE Bulletin, 39,* 3–7.

Knowles, M. S. (1990). Fostering competence in self-directed learning. In R. M. Smith (Ed.), *Learning to learn across the life span* (pp. 123–136). San Francisco: CA, Jossey-Bass.

Shapiro, N. S., & Levine, J. H. (1999). *Creating learning communities: A practical guide to winning support, organizing for change, and implementing programs.* San Francisco, CA: Jossey-Bass.

Watson, S. C. (2001). Institutional responses to adult students: Candid comments from students. *The Journal of Continuing Higher Education, 49* (2), 23–32.

10

The Entrepreneurial Response

Overview

As a result of ongoing and dynamic change, there is a fundamental conflict between the historic academy that has represented higher learning for well over four centuries and the academy of the 21st century. Adult learning strategies have largely been developed along the precise entrepreneurial precepts that are likely to thrive best in this change environment. Premier adult learning programs provide ample institutional models, given their entrepreneurial responses to the perpetual changes that have always characterized their existence—from accelerated course formats to credits obtained for prior learning initiatives, and from greater reliance upon technology (especially distance learning opportunities), to innovative partnerships that may redefine who the institution serves and how it provides that service. Some of the more notable creative solutions are provided here along with insights regarding how members of the academy may wish to generalize the process.

Some at-risk institutions are already showing signs that they may be the first casualties of the 21st century. For centuries, the academy has sought to maintain the status quo, so entrepreneurial strategies may pose a fundamental threat at many institutions. While change is inevitable on the campus, adult programs have typically played the primary role of change agent. This chapter demonstrates how, in the midst of rapid and profound change, many adult learning programs have managed to maintain integrity even as they respond to new and innovative market forces on their campus.

Introduction

As noted in earlier chapters, the academy and its members have long been unenthusiastic regarding the notion of entrepreneurialism. As a general precept, the term is frequently used on the campus pejoratively to denounce any practice or person seeking to introduce change into the ivory tower culture, even if it's practical or cost effective. In many ways, this tension underscores the elitist nature of the academy's roots. This, in turn, sets up a conflict on campus that is not likely to be resolved to the satisfaction of those seeking to maintain the status quo. After all, until very recently, higher education has been reserved for the privileged few. So change is at the very heart of this conflict—a sea change of such proportions that it is already impacting virtually every institution of higher learning in America. The evidence is pervasive and ubiquitous. Many faculty members and leaders are concerned with the notion of becoming more entrepreneurial. Benjamin Barber (2002, Spring), in his comments during the closing plenary talk at the Association of American Colleges and Universities' 2002 Annual Meeting, decries what has become commonplace in 21st century America:

> Commercialization and privatization go right across the board. You see them in every part of our society. You see cultural institutions increasingly dependent on corporate handouts. Because we will not fund the arts, the arts, too, like education have to make a profit. In our universities and colleges, scientists are now selling patents and making deals that the research they do will benefit not humanity and their students, but the shareholders of corporations, and so their research will otherwise be kept private. Again, most administrators welcome that because they don't have to raise faculty research budgets. The corporate world will take care of that. (p.26)

But the issues are even more complex and probably even more inevitable. To some degree, in the new knowledge-based society that defines the 21st century, every campus is undergoing some aspect of profound and tumultuous change. According to Herr (2001),

> Of the many forces altering the higher education industry, the following stand out as drivers of change:
>
> - a radical shift in the type of student and the sort of higher education desired;
> - an acceleration in the rate of knowledge accumulation that places a premium on lifetime education rather than on a one time undergraduate degree;

- increased demand for adult education and training;
- the adoption of new technologies;
- new web-based sources of information;
- evolution of the role of student as customer, teacher as content-provider and the institution as a business (for-profit or not-for-profit); and
- a restrained economy bordering on recession, which may drive more college graduates to stay in school or head for graduate programs. (pp. 11–12)

A revealing illustration is offered here to help the reader understand what may be at the core of the challenges posed by the items indicated above. At the very least is the consideration of "product" (like "customer," a term that seems to offend many academicians), as well as "service."

> In the aftermath of the tragedy of September 11, 2002, the government began evaluating what they had done well and what could have been improved. One federal agent stepped forward and, perhaps in a moment of frustration, revealed that some of her fellow agents were only now learning how to type or utilize modern technology of any sort. That revelation was shocking to many people who, in this information age, may have assumed that anyone involved in higher-level positions at least knows how to use a keyboard and almost everyone is at least nominally familiar with computers. What may have made the report more disturbing was that individuals in positions of responsibility had not managed to remain current—clearly, an implied expectation for almost any profession in today's world. Unfortunately, this is equally true on the college campus. For every innovative professor who is using various media, formats, and approaches in the classroom, there is probably a colleague on the same campus who still relies on the same yellowed, handwritten notes that he or she has been lecturing from for the past 20-plus years. This is the equivalent of a company making and selling typewriters in today's culture. Not only is the product outdated, it reflects an insensitivity to the market. Professors who rely

> on presenting the same basic lecture they delivered 20 years ago may be brilliant, but if they haven't made any attempt to understand their student's needs and orientation, they are underutilizing their resources and potential. Furthermore, while their "typewriter" may be really wonderful, it is still incompatible with the world we live in—as outmoded as the horse and carriage.

Until recently, education relied on a system that utilized the "endgame" concept. Once a learner completed a degree program, he or she moved to a different status: working in a career. Today, everyone is expected to continue learning throughout his or her entire life. In general, when a person stops pursuing new learning, he or she is likely to become stagnant and, based on the resulting loss or proficiencies, that person is no longer considered current or marketable. It is curious that some professors apparently do not see the need to remain current.

No Longer the Endgame

Historically, the academy has been built upon foundations that have proven to be reliable and stable—issues relating to the mission of the institution, the nature of the students served, the curriculum, and the role of the professorate. Now, however, a number of additions and changes have challenged the very core of the assumptions built into this model. In part, this is due to the radical influence of technology. Even as some professors staunchly refuse to integrate any form of technology (even the most benign) into their lives, many of their colleagues are making presentations in interactive classrooms and utilizing technology to bring learning to new, previously unimagined levels of sophistication and impact. In large part, these changes are the manifestation of market-driven initiatives coming out of an unparalleled level of competition among various institutions of higher learning. After all, when the practical shift took place from endgame to lifelong learner, the number of potential students grew exponentially. According to Aslanian (2001):

> Former students are future students. Adults in America today—and even more in the future—cannot stop learning. Colleges and other providers that meet their instructional needs have a built-in audience. Americans will have to keep coming back for more—more degrees, more courses, more

> certificates, and more workshops that will provide the skills and knowledge adults need to make successful transitions in their lives. The providers they return to will be those who are always there, always open, always welcoming. Americans today and in the future will not finish their education. They will be back, over and over, throughout their lifetimes. (p. 155)

Transforming the Academy

This situation is further compounded by the introduction of new components, notably the growing number of for-profit institutions and corporate universities that have further broadened the scope and range of the academy. As Newman (1999) notes, "New institutions, as well as the entrepreneurial response of existing institutions, are moving higher education from a system of state-based cartels to at least a partial open market" (p. 1). For-profit institutions such as the University of Phoenix have challenged the very foundation of higher education. As of February 28, 2002, the official enrollment for the University of Phoenix was 116,300 and still growing, according to Laura Palmer Noone, president of the institution (personal communication, June 12, 2002). What makes this figure so impressive is the exponential growth (29%) that has taken place in the 20 months since we had last spoken about enrollment figures. At the moment this book is being written, classes are offered at more than 116 campuses in 22 states (University of Phoenix, 2000), but these numbers will all probably expand even before this book is published. In the 26 years of its existence, the University of Phoenix has probably become the most dominant for-profit institution in the US. But there are many other new initiatives as well. For instance, many established universities have created their own dot-com for-profit parallel institutions, though some have already learned that this can be a risky and expensive undertaking. The number of companies that seek to gain portions of the market through strong business models and dedication to customer service continue to grow as well.

An article by Blumenstyk (2002) foresees continued long-term growth among the for-profit schools, based on a report from Eduventures Inc., a research and consulting firm in Boston.

> The report also predicts that the growth in for-profit colleges' revenues, which increased by 20 percent in 2001 over the

> previous year, will slow only slightly over the next few years—to 18 percent this year, 16 percent in 2003, and 15 percent in 2004. Eight companies account for more than 62 percent of all the revenues generated by for-profit colleges. (p. A27)

Levine (2000) emphasizes the importance of such initiatives while confirming the need for entrepreneurial strategies when he indicates a number of changes already underway in the academy: 1) "Changes in higher-education will become even more numerous and more diverse"; 2) "We should expect new brand names and a new hierarchy of quality in higher education institutions"; and 3) "Three types of colleges and universities are emerging: 'brick universities,' 'click universities,' and 'brick and click universities,' a combination of the first two" (p. B10). Consequently, according to a number of sources, a new institutional model is emerging based less on tradition and more on sensitivities to the market, new financial considerations, technology, and previously unimagined opportunities.

Corporate universities are still another unique option available to adult learners. The University Continuing Education Association (2002) confirms the phenomenal growth corporate universities have enjoyed:

> Corporate universities allow organizations to take a systematic approach to the learning and development of employees. The tenfold growth in the number of corporate universities between 1970 and 2000, and the better than 85 percent growth expected between 2000 and 2010, suggests the value of this training approach to the companies' bottom line. Though growth has clearly been robust, numbers may be somewhat misleading because there is no universally accepted definition of a corporate university. (p. 54)

In this highly charged environment, there are certain to be winners and losers—with a great deal at stake. Some schools will simply close and cease to exist. Competitors will absorb other schools in much the same manner as conglomerates have consumed mom-and-pop businesses and farms. At the core of this transformation is the need for an entrepreneurial response from any member of the academy that hopes to flourish in the future.

Models and Lessons Learned

Continuing education programs have been facing the harsh realities of such challenges for more than 50 years. Because they tend to be institutionally marginalized and usually lack the financial security of more established programs, they are more likely to be at risk so that their very existence relies on their flexibility, responsiveness, and willingness to think less conventionally. They are constantly forced to resolve these challenges with creativity and innovation—in other words, to be entrepreneurial.

What critics of this concept have failed to understand is that in the culture of the 21st century, maintaining the past is a luxury that no organization can afford. In the short span of the new century, many corporations have already learned this lesson the hard way as a precursor for members of the academy. What may be significantly different about this century is that there is no part of the academy that is exempt from this premise. To confirm the validity of this statement, one need only look as far as the leading institutions in America today to understand the profound and fully comprehensive nature of the change they are undergoing. Indeed, many of the most prestigious schools have understood the need for dynamic change and taken steps in their own transformation. In almost every instance, they have been consistent with or derivative of programs devoted to adult learners. For instance, the majority of technology-based learning is based on or gravitates toward the adult learner. When the Massachusetts Institute of Technology (MIT) began efforts to create public web pages for more than 2,000 of its courses (Young, 2001), even though it may have been groundbreaking in some sense, it was entirely consistent with adult programs that have already learned that they can strengthen their impact and attractiveness among adult learners by being as responsive and accessible as possible. MIT may have only presented itself as furthering its mission when it decided to create detailed web pages for nearly all of its courses and develop courseware tools that other institutions could use for free, but it demonstrated a level of innovative thinking and application that can only be seen as entrepreneurial as they gained worldwide attention and interest.

Many other schools, those who have less flexibility and financial wherewithal to achieve dynamic change, may have already begun to find themselves in an uncomfortable position. Typically, unlike their more prestigious counterparts, they simply lack the means to be forward thinking in their orientation (since they may have never needed to in the past).

Therefore, while some schools or faculty members may rail against entrepreneurialism, they are actually the frogs in the pot. So long as they resist change and continue their clamor to retain the academy of the past, they sit in that pot as the water gradually heats until it finally boils and cooks the frogs. As Lovett (2002) indicates, "It is time to focus on the resources we have, including public funds for instruction, research, and financial aid, and to rebuild the foundation of our higher education system on different premises" (p. 13). But members of the faculty may play an especially critical role in assisting the academy to move into a change mentality or orientation.

Regarding the internal strife often articulated among faculty:

> The situation could be very different today. Provided we have the will to embrace change, we have knowledge and resources never before available that can enable us to avoid this Hobsonian choice between quality and access, a choice alien to our belief in an intellectual meritocracy and to our democratic political culture. We can work to transform our colleges and universities into the best possible information-age organizations, transcending both our roots in the preindustrial age and our halfhearted adaptations of factory-style productions. (Lovett, 2002, p. 14)

Redefining the Academy Through Technology

It is through various aspects of technology where the distinction between the academy of the past and the 21st century is sharpest. The words of Gardner, Csikszentmihalyi, and Damon (2001) help us understand both the inevitability of technology on campus and why its use has largely fallen on the shoulders of adult learning programs:

> We are now entering an unprecedented era in which the economy requires people all over the world to become "knowledge workers." Entirely new tasks that require the constant and imaginative manipulation of symbols are providing employment to cohorts of computer programmers, software designers, bioengineers, and entrepreneurs knowledgeable enough to perceive opportunities in the evolving trends. Even those in professions seemingly remote from the cyber-revolution—say, the ministry or philanthropy—are

> affected by our computer-drenched society. Entering new territory always involves risk. As the forms of labor change, traditional safeguards for ensuring good work—from professional codes to trade unions—are no longer adequate. (pp. 15–16)

It is in this highly charged environment, where almost all adults are facing new levels of technological demands in the workplace and the redefinition of their tasks, that adult learners feel so compelled to upgrade their skills in order to provide themselves some measure of security and stability.

Even among institutions that have yet to make a strong commitment to utilizing technology to support instruction, the impact of technology becomes more pervasive each day. For instance, Young (2002) cited at least one college that already formally expects its faculty to "electronically acknowledge all student questions and assignments within 24 hours. Such requirements are rare at elite colleges and universities" (pp. A31–A32). But it does suggest that the academy is likely to function differently in the future, even at schools that don't currently envision any of the e-learning permutations as a part of their operation or mission.

Distance learning, blended learning, asynchronous learning, and any other delivery modes utilizing technology tend to be either directly offered through adult programs or aligned with the adult program. Aslanian (2001) suggests why this population may have particularly resonated to these media when she says:

> Finally, it may be that adults are the most computer literate of all students. Most occupations today require use of the computer. Therefore, the large majority of adult students who are employed are experienced in computer use. More important, they prefer it among all other distance options. (pp. 81–82)

When one considers that adult learners already comprise nearly 50% of all students enrolled in higher education, with continued expansion of these proportions anticipated, and given the graying of America, the academy cannot afford to ignore the impact of online learning. According to the University Continuing Education Association (2002):

> Online education is one way to alleviate the crush of postsecondary enrollments that will overwhelm many institutions in

> the next several years. Though not a complete solution, investing in the infrastructure to deliver high quality distance education is more cost- and time-effective than building the necessary classrooms and hiring sufficient faculty resources to meet the coming demand. (p. 71)

The Competitive Factor

As the competition for students continues to increase and traditional funding sources continue to decline, more and more schools are likely to succumb to the market pressures associated with for-profit institutions and other business practices. If change is the catalyst that has impelled the academy in the first place, responsiveness and sensitivity to the needs of customers is likely to be the most notable shift in strategy. Again, this is a derivative of entrepreneurial thinking, as noted by Newman (1999):

> If the process of change in higher education, pressed by these new forces, continues in the general direction it is headed; if academic and political leaders work together to help steer the process of change into constructive channels; and if care is taken to ensure the changes do not undercut essential characteristics of higher education, the United States could be headed for a different and more effective system. Such a system of higher education might be:
>
> - More focused on the learner and less on the institution.
> - More dependent on measures of competency than seat time.
> - More focused on effective pedagogy, with imaginative use of technology to enhance this focus.
> - More mixed (public/private, private/nonprofit, virtual/traditional).
> - More dependent on market forces (new suppliers, old institutions doing new things, old boundaries obliterated).
> - More responsive to societal needs as increased competitive pressures force institutions to address longstanding issues, such as cost and productivity, the assurance of quality and focus on learners' needs. (pp. 7–8)

The Faculty Component

Faculty members may be more challenged by this change than any other campus stakeholders. Traditionalists see every aspect of their heritage disappearing in the academy of the 21st century—from fixed desks and cloned lectures derived from yellowed notes to movable formats and interactive classrooms. As some faculty members continue to rely on their typewriters or pens and eschew computers for any part of their existence, they are also likely to rebuff any elements of the new century. In their dissatisfaction with these changes, they are likely to echo McBride (2002) who noted:

> I would guess that the future holds less in the way of political crisis and more in the way of continued technological revolution. If so, then no teacher will be able to compete with the computer and university professors may simply become, along with the World Wide Web, one more resource. Personableness will not be required, and might even become irrelevant (or a pedagogical value affordable only at the most elite institutions). (p. B5)

Issues relating to distance learning and technology will not be the only factors that contribute to a significantly changed academy in the 21st century. Other notable characteristics of continuing education programs that have endured for decades may also provide special insights for the academy as well.

For instance, Halfond (2002) touches upon the dramatic role continuing education has taken in helping to challenge the one-teaching-style-fits-all approach many instructors are apt to utilize in their traditional classes.

> As anyone knows who has experienced the challenge of maintaining student enthusiasm during marathon classes, a long class is not simply a matter of stacking the content of shorter classes consecutively. It takes great teaching skill to motivate students for the sixth hour of a six-hour Saturday class. It takes a multimedia concept of learning to appreciate how to script an intensive course. The more concentrated courses, the higher the stakes. Teaching is more challenging, the quality of the facilities more important, and the motivation of the students critical. Some of the most radical experiments in higher

> learning are now being conducted in our units by amateur (as opposed to career) faculty whom we hire to teach adults at a distance, on weekends, in off-campus settings. (p. 52)

Of course, while faculty members who have worked closely and successfully with adult learners understand the validity of Halfond's comments, other faculty members are likely to hear or see them as inflammatory. The academy still has a long journey to complete the transformation envisioned among the better adult learner programs. Perhaps, however, greater attention is being paid to this notion than ever before. As Halfond (2002) points out:

> The nontraditional role of continuing education had previously pushed much of our business to the periphery of our institutions. However, we are now in the vanguard, not only in addressing the lifelong learning needs of society and using a variety of professionals to serve as faculty, but by experimenting with the very process of learning itself. (p. 52)

One of the most fascinating aspects in the future of higher education will tell whether the academy fully recognizes and appreciates the virtues associated with adult learner programs.

Accelerated Learning: Not Just Talking Faster

Although a flurry of research has been applied to the topic of accelerated learning during the past decade, many faculty members remain skeptical of any option that involves reduced seat time. The notion that a five- or eight-week course can achieve equivalency with the more conventional term-long class that meets over an extended period remains highly controversial. Indeed, this tends to be one of the more inflammatory and contentious issues between the academy's traditionalists and those professors who have learned that the same outcomes can be achieved (and sometimes even surpassed) in accelerated formats.

Donaldson and Graham (2002) have identified four types of issues related to accelerated programs:

1) ***Outcomes.*** Are outcomes from accelerated programs comparable to those of conventional programs? What kinds of learning outcomes do

adults experience? How satisfied are adults with accelerated programs and why?

2) ***Learning Environment.*** Are course format changes based on strategies that enhance student learning or designed solely to attract more student enrollments? Can adults accomplish the work necessary outside of class with busy lifestyles, and if not, what is being displaced? What broader characteristics of the learning environment enhance or impede learning?

3) ***Student Characteristics.*** What factors associated with the learners themselves influence learning in accelerated programs? How do these factors enhance or impede learning and why?

4) ***Administrative and Curricular Policy.*** Are policies for accelerated programs guided by current academic policies and input from the regular college faculty? Do the traditional faculty members play a critical role in shaping the policies for accelerated degree programs? (p. 2)

The results of their study produced suggestions for designing accelerated programs based on principles of adult learning:

Prior Experience and Personal Biographies

1) Instructors should value what learners already know, help them to articulate and make it explicit, and help them evaluate its quality.

2) Instructors should design instructional strategies and techniques, as well as class projects, to connect with and build upon what learners already know.

3) Instructors should be sensitive to how adults evaluate themselves as learners and should see their participation in accelerated programs as opportunities for adults to reassess themselves.

Psycho-social and Value Orientations

1) Instructors should help learners see how accelerated courses or programs differ from conventional formats and how the format itself can "support" and "push" them to completion.

2) Administrators and instructors can enhance adult motivation by demonstrating that accelerated programs foster relatively fast outcomes.

3) Administrators and instructors should emphasize that accelerated programs can lead to depth, as opposed to breadth, of coverage and knowledge.

4) Administrators and instructors should employ strategies to reduce psychological distress.

The Connecting Classroom

1) Any unnecessary content or "busy work" should be eliminated from the accelerated format.

2) Instructors should design the classroom environment so that adult students can explain and translate knowledge for other learners.

3) Expertise across multiple cultures and communities of practice should be recognized, valued, and used in instruction.

4) Instruction should be adjusted to permit learners to connect what they are learning in and out of class.

5) The classroom should be viewed as a multicultural place for learners in the broader world rather than a unicultural world of the collegiate environment.

Adult Cognition

1) Instructors should design activities or assignments that draw out existing knowledge.

2) Instructors should provide classroom experiences that allow adults to confront previous mental conceptions of the new material.

3) Instructors should design course activities and assignments that integrate the content with students' work.

4) Instructors should recognize that the relevancy of new knowledge is a key feature for adult learners.

5) Instructors should allow learners' needs and the course format to dictate the amount of time spent on the different elements of the course.

Life-World Environment

1) Learning time can be used most efficiently by integrating learning and knowledge use with learners' roles at work, in the family, and in the community.

2) The classroom climate and the organization for learning (e.g., use of cohorts, group projects) can offer social support and genuine caring for all learners.

3) An orientation should provide learners with accurate information about the program and strategies for renegotiating their life roles while in the program.

College Outcomes for Adults

1) Program goals should include both mastery and ownership of knowledge.

2) Accelerated programs should result, at minimum, in elaboration of life-worlds knowledge structures. Preferably, they should result in integrative, transformative learning.

Administration and Curriculum

1) The college should reduce or eliminate administrative trivia.

2) The college should articulate course format and structure clearly from the beginning so adult students are aware of deadlines and assignments.

3) Students should have multiple entry points to access material.

4) The college should vary the schedule for accelerated programs (such as the number of weeks, contact hours, breaks between sessions, completion times) according to the course content, type of knowledge, variability of learners' preexisting knowledge, etc.

5) Practitioners with strong academic knowledge and the ability to connect learning, practice, and existing student knowledge are desirable as instructors in adult programs.

6) Accelerated course content should align closely with the campus curriculum and subsequent courses students may take.

7) Likewise, schools must align curriculum to the overall program structure.

8) Decisions about who establishes courses' standards must be clearly articulated. Curriculum decisions should be made by committees of faculty members and should not be made by programmers or administrative officials.

9) Readings assigned prior to the official "start" of a course and advance organizers used prior to formal instruction can become effective ways to make the best use of limited class time in accelerated programs.

10) Faculty development is an essential strategy in accelerated programming. (pp. 8–11)

Although the guidelines contained in the article are included here, the valuable explications provided by the authors are not. Anyone seeking further details concerning accelerated degree programs or courses is encouraged to utilize this article.

Technology at the Core of the Institution

Instructors and administrators primarily involved with adult learning are, by the very nature of their students, change agents. The entrepreneurial response required for this student population relates to their dynamic lifestyle and experiences beyond the campus. Adult learners constantly bring new experiences into their classroom—experiences primarily based on their recent work and life challenges. Adult learner programs and classes tend to be much more organic in their development as the needs of the students are likely to change more dramatically than for those of their younger classmates, where theoretical rather than practical applications are apt to be emphasized. The result is that instructors for adult learners typically find themselves facing a kaleidoscope of change since that is at the very core of the adult learner experience. In many applications, the benefits derived from this experience tend to relate to technology, since this faculty, demonstrating greater flexibility, may be more open to new applications. That is, faculty members who work frequently with adults generally tend to be less reluctant to use technology. This is particularly noteworthy since, according to the University Continuing Education Association (2002), "the International Data Corporation predicts that by 2005, 90%

of all higher education institutions will have e-learning programs" (p. 71). On the other hand, "Even if e-learning fails to reach the optimistic goals of its proponents, the entrepreneurial attitude will have changed the landscape" (Herr, 2001, p. 11).

From the other side of the equation, King (2002), in her research concerning the changes faculty in adult programs experienced by using technology in their teaching and learning, revealed that:

> Learning and using educational technology is a prime occasion for faculty to reflect on their practice, ask hard questions, and step aside from familiar and comfortable teaching and learning paradigms. As faculty learn technology, many of them begin to recast their concepts and practices of educational processes. While educational organizations are pressed to integrate technology, it is evident that they may also be able to experience educational change and perhaps develop a seedbed for educational reform. (p. 35)

This helps confirm a position held by Altschuler and McClure (2002) who noted the need for a comprehensive technology plan based on three elements: 1) helping faculty members to use technology to redesign their courses and create new ones, 2) incorporating technology in their classrooms, and 3) improving the technological infrastructure throughout the institution. As they indicate: "A plan should first consider how to make faculty members aware of the new pedagogical possibilities available through technology" (B16).

But it is the entrepreneurial impulse related to the use of technology that continues to propel the academy forward:

> How can institutions produce courses for veterinarians in large-animal clinics and systems engineers working for General Motors if most of the faculty members qualified to teach them are unfamiliar with the technology, less than passionate about continuing education, and skeptical about the academic quality of material in courses designed primarily to make a profit? (p. B16)

Note the implications built into this question. Obviously, few schools are designed to respond to either the needs of veterinary students or systems engineers. But the concepts hold true, regardless of the specificity of the area of study. Likewise, note the prominence of continuing education in this statement (as confirmed with "passionate about continuing education"). Of course, at the very heart of the matter are those final four words that account for the inevitability of increasing technology use on campus: "to make a profit." It has largely fallen to programs in continuing education to blaze the trail on behalf of the academy when it comes to the use of technology. Just as the ultimate use of technology as an everyday part of learning for all students is inevitable, working out the details will largely fall to adult learner programs. Even if a campus doesn't offer an adult learner program, the lessons they are likely to draw from will have been largely derived from adult programs somewhere.

Prior Learning Assessment and Other Shortcuts

One other practice associated with adult learning—prior learning assessment—draws its earliest practice from 19th century Britain during the Industrial Revolution, when the University of London was first opened to the public in 1836. This event caused a restructuring of higher education according to Thorstein Veblen (as cited in Pittman, 2002), since this event changed the emphasis of education from apprenticeship and on-the-job training to the development of individual intelligence and general knowledge. As Pittman (2002) notes:

> England's ancient and hallowed universities were singularly unequipped to serve this change in societal demand. They had no means of—and little interest in—serving great numbers of adults, often working people, for whom higher education had become a necessity. (p. 59)

By 1858, a revised charter allowed this institution to:

> examine any candidates who presented themselves, both in the British Isles and sites around the Empire. Neither residence nor evidence of formal preparation of any kind was demanded. Candidates with passing scores, regardless of the manner in which they prepared themselves, would receive a degree. (p. 59)

Today's equivalent can be found dispersed over a wide range of options. From an institutional perspective, Excelsior College (formerly

Regents College) appears to be the modern equivalent of the original University of London, except that all activities are accomplished through various permutations of distance education. (For a detailed description of this school, see Maehl, 2000, pp. 116–127). In the 21st century, this program may represent the fullest extent of accessibility to all members of the general public

Although there are a number of external tests that many schools utilize for adult learners to acquire credit for what they know (CLEP, ACE, DANTE, Excelsior College Examinations), portfolio-based assessment of prior learning is the most common individualized assessment method. As previously noted, the Council for Adult and Experiential Learning (CAEL) has led the field in this practice. Its publication of the book *Assessing Learning: Standards, Principles, and Procedures* (Whitaker, 1989) has established the gold standard for this practice. Unfortunately, not all adult programs have always practiced a rigorous, reliable, and valid assessment of the student's presentation. As Arnold (2002) notes:

> To achieve reliability and validity in a program's assessment process, one must make sure that the methods and procedures in place are dependable and credible. Students, faculty, and administrators want to see evidence that the process can be trusted to produce accurate and fair assessments of student learning. (p. 66)

Accrediting consultants or evaluators and agencies should be added to this list as well. The use of any of these instruments has made acquiring credits for what they've previously learned significantly more accessible to adult learners. This is simply another example of how adult programs have developed innovative practices while maintaining high standards.

Often—perhaps too often—colleges and universities want to have their cake and eat it too when it comes to their adult programs. Administrators and trustees appreciate the income and cost effectiveness associated with such programs, but frequently are reluctant to support some of the more entrepreneurial initiatives associated with them. This is more likely to happen when it comes to marketing, but it can be a problem with any aspect of the program. In this case, Laura, the new director of

an adult division at Staid University, is trying to breathe fire into a program that has been gradually declining in its enrollment. Unfortunately, Ted, the president of the school, has begun to feel as though her ideas are a threat to the image and tradition of the institution. As a result, the two individuals have begun to find themselves at odds with one another.

Case Study: Ted and Laura

Laura Midnight came to Staid University (SU) like a knight in shining armor ready to save the institution from the steady decline in enrollment the adult program had experienced during the past five years. She brought with her a rich background, having experienced success in three careers before coming to higher education. Indeed, it was her success as a consultant and businesswoman (in two different fields) that first led her to adult learning in higher education. When she accepted her first position as director of a modest continuing education program, her boss, a woman who had been in higher education her entire career, set rather moderate objectives for Laura and the program. When she doubled those goals, it was apparent that Laura had some special skills to help her in this field. It was just this sort of continued success she had enjoyed at two other schools that helped convince Ted Borg, president at SU, that Laura could turn the SU adult program around and regain the high enrollments of adult learners the school had once enjoyed. In fact, this was the very mandate Ted gave Laura: "You're the expert—I want you to revitalize the adult program at SU!"

Initially, Laura needed to stop the bleeding, as one of her staff described it, and reverse the enrollment pattern. Laura's response to this challenge was to make a number of minor modifications regarding SU's current adult learners. She was able to initiate some minor changes after utilizing a simple survey that helped her determine what SU's adult learners considered their biggest problems and greatest needs. She was able to make a number of quick adjustments that didn't significantly alter SU's orientation toward adult learners but sent a clear message to the students that they were being listened to. By the end of Laura's first year, after a great deal of hard work, the adult program showed signs of new vitality and, for the first time in many years, the adult enrollment didn't significantly decline.

But Laura knew from experience that her work so far had only focused on remedial issues and that the true transformation Ted continued to ask about ("How soon do you think we will see an increase in enrollment for the adult program?") would require a different approach. So far, Laura had only helped provide a strong foundation for the new program, but much of the creative work was still to be addressed. It was in the middle stages of this next phase where the tension began to grow between Ted and Laura.

Based on all the research and demographic information Laura had collected, one of the first interventions her division would undertake came from the new web page they wanted to construct. Although the page would be contained within the SU web site, Laura wanted to create a page she described as adult-friendly. Indeed, she and her staff did extensive surveys and observations to determine what the adult learners at SU preferred. For instance, because the vast majority of her students were female and their average age was over 35, the current and potential SU adult learners expressed a preference for a page that was a little more on the cute side rather than the conservative image favored by the school. As Laura continued to field-test various pages, she found that the adult learners tended to resonate a great deal more to an image that was adult-friendly and reassuring. She also discovered that the images that SU had selected for their web page did not provide the sense of security and accessibility the adult students expressed a preference for. Since her mandate had been to increase enrollment, her decision seemed simple: offer the web page that showed the best positive response among potential students.

Unfortunately, Ted saw the page in an entirely different perspective. "The cute little figures you have used on your web page are totally incompatible with the image of this institution," he told Laura at their first meeting after the page appeared. "You've also used bright colors and even humor in your message—none of the kinds of displays normally associated with SU or its message! In fact, your page diminishes how people are likely to look at us."

When Laura tried to respond by pointing out all the market research and field-testing they had already done with their target population, Ted was simply not willing to be persuaded. "Look Laura," he responded, "I've already heard from two of the trustees who are uncomfortable with the images your division is showing on the web. These gentlemen contribute a large sum of money to the institution each year—they have been associated with SU for many years. I simply can't support you marketing your program with cute figures and bright colors."

Although Laura was not thrilled by this conversation and continued to privately disagree with Ted on his position, she knew there were no options available to her in this instance. When she returned to her office that day, there were two flyers that had come in the mail that day that caught her attention. Although they both advertised one-day seminars, one used cartoon figures extensively, both to set a tone and to illustrate points that would be covered in the presentation. The other flyer used a few photographs, but its overall format was more formal and reserved. Laura's initial response was more favorable to the first but as she continued to look at both flyers, she began to see how she might be able to comply with Ted's request and still produce a page that would appeal to her target adult learners at the same time.

At first glance, when you look at the SU web page today, there isn't anything that seems remarkable about the pages devoted to the adult learner. Visually, they look similar to all the other pages, in terms of the color and design format. But as your comparison becomes more in-depth, you begin to notice that the contents of the adult learner pages are much more extensive. Indeed, these web pages quickly and efficiently lead adult students and potential adult students to every possible topic or question. They are based on optimum service to the student. You notice that the information is updated with all the most current details. There are a number of links that enable the adult learners to accomplish activities such as access future schedules, register, audit their grades, determine their progress toward graduation, etc. that exceed what their daytime classmates can do.

Privately, Laura remains convinced that if her division had been able to sustain the original web page, their enrollments might easily surpass the modest success they have enjoyed so far. At the same time, she is thankful that, through other entrepreneurial initiatives, she has at least been able to offer adult learners some incentives for coming to SU (such as valet parking, a wide range of accelerated learning schedule formats, and free coffee during breaks). These have captured some of her more innovative concepts and reminded her that a portion of being entrepreneurial is being perseverant and persistent. And whenever she may feel a bit frustrated, she plays a scene in her head where she walks into Ted's office to tell him about the new billboard advertising campaign she envisions. The fantasy scream from Ted always elicits a quiet little smile on Laura's face.

● ● ● ● ●

Conclusion

Sustaining the status quo in the academy has become an art form. But in the 21st century, it is the equivalent of arranging the deck chairs for the *Titanic.* There are too many stories that support the boiling frog principle. For instance, one school I know of assembled the faculty of an at-risk department to express their exigency and discuss their options. The chair noted that, due to decreased enrollment, the members of the department would all need to actively participate in some outreach efforts and make other comparable efforts or they faced losing their major and, for most of them, their jobs. Almost as a single voice, they responded that their job didn't include such activities and if that meant closing the department, so be it. I've often wondered whether they later regretted their position once the department was permanently closed.

When it comes to notable factors that may have made the greatest impact, I suspect that what has thrown the academy into disarray as much as any single factor in the past 30 years may be the University of Phoenix. There have been for-profit proprietary schools around for many years, so it wasn't just a new for-profit offering that created the uproar. Their approach, however, was unlike anything the academy had seen before. The University of Phoenix and their parent company, the Apollo Group, have altered the landscape of higher education forever, especially when it comes to the entrepreneurial spirit and imagination they have applied to higher education.

My purpose here is not to serve as a cheerleader on their behalf. They are so narrowly defined that they are marginal (albeit successful) at best, and they really don't need me to speak in their behalf—the immensity of their impact is self-evident. But there have been a number of memorable aspects of their existence that I have found impressive, far-reaching, and noteworthy.

I was fortunate enough in 2000 to have been selected as a Management and Leadership in Education fellow in the Harvard University Institute for

Higher Education program offered each summer to a select group of college administrators. During the two-week session, we were introduced to a vast array of readings and speakers, but there was a special level of energy and engagement on the morning that Laura Palmer Noone, then provost of the University of Phoenix (UOP), was the guest speaker. Although the participants didn't outright attack her during her presentation about UOP, they were ready to challenge virtually every aspect of the program. While they had been slightly reserved and informal in their interaction with all other speakers, there was a level of intensity during this presentation that was palpable. Students sat on the edges of their seats and vied with their classmates to ask the next question or make the next observation. It was electric!

We all discovered that the majority of UOP students are not pursuing their studies via distance learning (perhaps the leading misconception about the program). We also learned that UOP had created a faculty development piece that is the envy of all but a few institutions within the academy. UOP had not only passed (with high marks) the almost-annual accreditation visits they have experienced since their beginning, but that they must also pass regulations set out by the New York Stock Exchange (an additional challenge most of our schools never face). The innovations and concept of the UOP program are so extensive it's impossible to list them all here, but it gave us all a peek at what an entrepreneurial approach to higher learning might entail.

I was impressed with how well Dr. Palmer Noone handled the near hostility expressed by some of my classmates. I was also impressed by the nature of the energy and enmity as well. This may have been the first moment I fully realized what a threat entrepreneurialism may be to so many in the academy. There was never another moment during the program where everyone was quite so aggressive.

Because UOP was scheduled to open a campus near my school in the Cleveland area the upcoming fall, I received from Dr. Mark Collier, president of Baldwin-Wallace College, approval to ask Dr. Palmer Noone if she would consider making a presentation on our campus to leaders and members of the community when she was in town for the UOP/Cleveland opening. She graciously accepted and generously gave two versions of her presentation: one for department chairs and campus leaders as part of a dinner program the night before, and again on the next day to the broader community. In both cases, I observed the same level of intensity—the near animosity associated with the UOP program being demonstrated by some of the good people in the audience who seemed to be offended by what they heard. Upon consideration, I came to believe that what they were hearing ran contrary to many (if not all) of their preconceptions about the role and mission of the academy. And who could blame them? It is troublesome when you first encounter really new ideas that challenge the core of your beliefs. It was a stunning example of how powerful the threat of change can be to those who don't welcome and embrace it.

Since then, the director of the local UOP and I have agreed that even though we are both seeking adult learners, our programs offer such different approaches on how adult learners acquire their learning (i.e., as a member of a cohort group in lockstep as opposed to an individual with a wide range of scheduling options) that we are not in direct competition with one another. However, during those two presentations, many people from various institutions all behaved as though they were looking at their school's biggest competitor.

If UOP embodies change and the entrepreneurial spirit, it is simply leading (and sometimes following) the adult learner programs' parade. The academy is facing greater challenges than it ever has in the past. It is interesting to consider, however, that few schools are likely to be at the level of risk that most adult programs face on an almost daily basis. In fact, it is probably that living on the edge experience that makes the entrepreneurial approach so compelling for these programs in the first place.

Any school that believes it is somehow exempt from the need to be entrepreneurial need only look at how many successful corporations have ceased to exist during the short period of this century, while others have radically changed their mission or mode of doing business in order to remain competitive. Schools should pay close attention to business models during this century, not because the business models are inherently better, but because there are lessons to be learned—both in their successes and failures. Businesses or schools who lose the ability to respond to the needs of their constituents put themselves at risk. Adult programs learn this lesson early and well or they are likely to find themselves in jeopardy. There are plentiful lessons to be learned from this source for those institutions that are willing to consult their adult programs.

References

Altschuler, G. C., & McClure, P. (2002, January 18)....and colleges must create technology. *The Chronicle of Higher Education,* pp. B16–B17.

Arnold, T. (2002, Spring). Reliability and validity in assuring quality for prior learning assessment. *The Journal of Continuing Higher Education, 50* (2), 64–66.

Aslanian, C. (2001). *Adult students today.* Washington, DC: The College Board.

Barber, B. R. (2002, Spring). The educated student: Global citizen or global consumer? *Liberal Education, 88* (2), 22–28.

Blumenstyk, G. (2002, June 28). Companies in the 'education industry' get optimistic revenue predictions. *The Chronicle of Higher Education,* p. A27.

Donaldson, J. F., & Graham, S. W. (2002, Spring). Accelerated degree programs: Design and policy implications. *The Journal of Continuing Higher Education, 50* (2), 2–13.

Gardner, H., Csikszentmihalyi, M., & Damon, W. (2001). *Good work: When excellence and ethics meet.* New York, NY: Basic Books.

Halfond, J. A. (2002, Spring). Further reflections on teaching. *The Journal of Continuing Higher Education, 50* (2), 50–52.

Herr, L. K. (2001, Winter). Survival in the new marketplace. *Assessment and Accountability Forum, 11* (4), 11–12, 18.

King, K. P. (2002, Spring). Technology catalyzing change in how faculty teach and learn. *The Journal of Continuing Higher Education, 50* (2), 26–37.

Levine, A. E. (2000, October). The future of colleges: Nine inevitable changes. *The Chronicle of Higher Education,* p. B10–B11.

Lovett, C. M. (2002, March/April). Cracks in the bedrock: Can U.S. higher education remain number one? *Change,* 11–15.

Maehl, W. H. (2000). *Lifelong learning at its best: Innovative practices in adult credit programs.* San Francisco, CA: Jossey-Bass.

McBride, T. (2002, May 31). Curiously average: The way we teach. *The Chronicle of Higher Education,* p. B5.

Newman, F. (1999, March 5). *The transformation of American higher education.* Retrieved August 22, 2001, from http://www.futuresproject.org/publications/american_education.pdf

Pittman, V. (2002, Spring). Context v. content: An enduring battle in distance education. *The Journal of Continuing Higher Education, 50* (2), 59–60.

University Continuing Education Association. (2002). *Lifelong learning trends.* Washington, DC: Author.

University of Phoenix. (2000). *Yes, you can do this.* Retrieved June 12, 2002, from http://www.phoenix.edu

Whitaker, U. (1989). *Assessing learning: Standards, principles & procedures.* Philadelphia, PA: Council for Adult and Experiential Learning.

Young, J. R. (2001, December 14). MIT begins effort to create public web pages for more than 2,000 of its courses. *The Chronicle of Higher Education,* p. A34.

Young, J. R. (2002, May 31). The 24-hour professor. *The Chronicle of Higher Education,* pp. A31–A33.

Part Four

Lifelong Learning: Education Is No Longer an Endgame

11

Graduation Is Only a Way Station in the Lifelong Learning Journey

Overview

In a culture that expects the typical traditional student who graduates from college to experience six to seven career choices in his or her lifetime, no person can afford to think of his or her education as having been completed. Ongoing learning experiences dominate the workplace and define any individual's future so long as he or she seeks advancement and marketability. While this is a fairly recent trend in higher education, it emphasizes that learning should be perceived as part of a continuum. Although this continuum is defined on some campuses as extending from the traditional entry point until retirement, other schools broaden their definition to include all students from birth to the end of life.

The justification for lifelong learning programs, offering a full range of options to support higher education, begins with the realization that no school can afford to merely focus on the traditional 18- to 22-year-old student any longer. In addition, if the school has a commitment to members of its community, it will need to deliver different formats and ways of learning to ensure that all constituents are receiving their fair share.

Introduction

The term "paradigm shift" has become a part of the jargon in higher education. Because the term has often been applied as a synonym for change, it has become so overused that it has largely lost its impact or effectiveness. But, in the academy of the 21st century, it is hard to imagine using any other term to describe the vast changes that are associated with the concept of lifelong learning.

Lifelong learning has become another piece of educational jargon that has emerged throughout the academy in recent times. In its more common usage, it has denoted an extension of undergraduate work, typically at the graduate level. But when one makes a simple comparison with college or university mission statements from the previous decade, it is obvious that the term has gained fashion in its broader applications at many institutions in recent years. However, there is less evidence that schools are offering "cradle to grave" instruction for all learners or that doing so is even consistent with their mission or strategic plans. Instead, the term is consistently used to suggest how colleges and universities seek to support their students in today's world. Twenty-first century college graduates are routinely informed that they are likely to change careers six or seven times during their life. As a result, lifelong learning is a term used to convey how the institution is trying to help these students as they seek to recycle their education and remain current in an ever-changing environment.

The first chapter of this book outlined a number of reasons why adult learners are important to colleges or universities in the 21st century. Interestingly enough, the primary focus of that chapter—and most of the subsequent chapters—examined what might be thought of as the "conventional" adult learner who has studied on many school campuses during recent decades. But the lifelong learning movement may extend well beyond that original paradigm. On the other hand, the term remains somewhat ambiguous since it has many interpretations. In an effort to optimize continuity and serve members of their community, some schools are systematically creating programs that respond to all learners. For instance, Chapter 8 examines how schools may wish to address the learning needs of the elderly population and why such a commitment makes good institutional sense. But leaders of authentic, full-range institutions, wanting to serve all learners, are likely to recognize how learning from cradle to grave should be considered seamless. Such visionary leaders are likely to believe that the mission of his or her institution includes the obligation to respond to the greater need of all members of the community. Ultimately, these institutions are likely to be recognized as a rich, rigorous, and primary resource for all learners, regardless of their age. Interestingly, such a strategy and commitment places a greater onus on the learner than on the teacher, but it also reinforces the notion that the function of the academy is to serve as an enriched learning center for the entire community.

Cross (1999) provides a clear illustration of the 21st century lifelong learner.

> What we really need for workers and citizens of the twenty-first century is people who can conduct a lifelong conversation between their own experience and learning—who can use their experience to enhance learning and their learning to enrich application. Employers insist that they need workers who can think and analyze problems on the job. This is a different skill demand from the old manufacturing format of training workers to apply knowledge gained in school to the job. Today, there are so many different jobs, and they change so rapidly, that training for specific jobs has become largely irrelevant. Employers want workers who can think, analyze problems, critique solutions, and perhaps most importantly continue to learn to do their jobs better. That will require the ability to learn from experience, to constantly reflect on what has been learned, to experiment with alternatives, and to evaluate the outcomes. (p. 21)

It is this vision of lifelong learning as it applies to the 21st century employee that is most likely to resonate with the academy in general. This vision also strengthens the justification of adult learning programs specifically, even prior to any consideration of how an institution can respond to the learning needs of the remainder of the community.

Current Examples of Practice

In application, what the virtual concept of lifelong learning suggests, or perhaps confirms, since practically every chapter in this book has dealt with some aspects of this term as it is described above, is that adult learning programs are well-suited and often specifically designed to meet the learning needs of all constituents throughout their lives. Typically, this suggests that continuing education programs are more likely to perceive all students as part of their domain. With the possible exception of community colleges, this perception is what marks these programs as distinctive from the remainder of the academy, who are likely to define the students they serve more narrowly.

Furthermore, in addition to this expanded perspective regarding target student population, there is also another common thread that is woven throughout the descriptions of successful programs: Stakeholders in continuing education value responsiveness to their clientele. This helps us to understand how continuing education programs tend to be at the cutting edge of identifying the changing needs of their target population (and, indeed, even defining who that population might be in the future). According to Knox (1990):

> One distinctive characteristic of the professional as learner is having a responsible occupational position based on substantial formal education and ability. Many continuing professional education activities seek to deliver recent information regarding specialized aspects of a complex knowledge base and practice profile. A holistic view of professionals as self-directed and informed consumers of continuing professional education is also desirable. (p. 240)

This often suggests, therefore, that adult learner programs think about learning in a different context than the remainder of the academy. Specifically, these programs are likely to generate learning situations that can be either directly applied in the workplace or can be generalized for future applications. As such, these activities reflect a growing expectation among students of all ages that their learning will provide them with skills and a knowledge base that, first and foremost, is designed to support them in the workplace for the future.

A subset of the responsiveness valued among adult learners relates to service. Successful adult learner programs often seek to provide a consistently high level of world-class service, perhaps in part due to the extreme level of competitiveness that many adult programs experience and in part due to the elevated expectations of the adult learners. Specifically, Bash and Martyn (2000) identified a number of characteristics that they employed and integrated into their program in order to achieve this level of service:

- The organization's cultural climate reflects a commitment to meeting and exceeding customer expectations.

- Senior leaders demonstrate by example the organization's commitment to exceptional courtesy.
- Employees are empowered to fully meet the needs of their customers.
- Courtesy is practiced by everyone throughout the entire organization.
- Specific and ongoing training in courtesy is provided.
- Formal and informal screening techniques are used to hire employees with exceptional skills in courtesy.
- The organization establishes systems to measure the value of its services to customers.
- There is zero tolerance for discourteous service. (p. 4)

These characteristics are overt signals that institutions send out for adult learners to help reinforce the perception that the program is adult learner focused. When consistently applied, evidence suggests that programs utilizing these strategies generate high levels of customer satisfaction and support. For schools that expect to "recycle" their students via certificates, workshops, etc., the level of satisfaction these strategies are likely to engender may pay substantial dividends in the long run, making them investment strategies. Although they may seem benign in an isolated context, when applied to the visionary projections provided in the next section of this chapter, such strategies make perfect sense as a safeguard against the possibility of declining enrollments.

EDUCATIONAL PASSPORTS, CRADLE TO ROCKER, ACTIVE LEARNING

Perhaps one of the most interesting facets of lifelong learning is that it is a term that has many different manifestations and applications. In one provocative and fascinating example, Levine (2000) notes that:

> *Degrees will wither in importance* [italics added]. Today, the meaning of a degree varies in content and quality, depending on the college. In essence, we offer thousands of different degrees, even if they are called by the same name. A degree now signifies a period of successful college attendance; the

> class rank indicates the relative success of the student; and the name of the college marks the quality of the degree.
>
> However, with the change in emphasis from institutional process to educational outcomes, degrees will become far less meaningful. A transcript of each student's competencies, including the specific information that the student knows or the skills that he or she can perform will be far more desirable. (p. B10)

Furthermore, Levine (2000) also states that, as both a logical consequence of the withering of importance associated with degrees and the growing emphasis on lifelong learning:

> *Every person will have an educational passport* [italics added]. In the future, each person's education will occur not only in a cornucopia of different settings and geographic locales, but also via a plethora of different educational providers. As traditional degrees lose importance, the nation will need to establish a central bureau that records each person's educational achievements—however and wherever they were gained—and that provides documentation. Such an educational passport, or portfolio, will record a student's lifetime educational history. (p. B11)

For many years, Ellen was often described as self-made, having been part of a generation that could achieve a certain level of success in business without benefit of a formal education. In her case, she faced the additional challenge of competing in a business setting that was considered predominantly part of a man's world. Because she was tough (though polished), street smart (with wisdom beyond her years), and energetic (possessing a work ethic that would define her throughout her life), she had managed to accomplish an impressive array of achievements. As full partner in a highly successful business, there's a possibility that Ellen might not have ever pursued a college degree, but events in her life ultimately contributed to her decision that she couldn't afford not to have a degree, even if she would be near retirement age by the time she completed her studies. This was a decision that would alter her life forever.

Ellen serves to remind us that, while learning takes many forms, it's never too late and the experience is capable of making powerful transformations.

Case Study: Ellen

If you were to meet Ellen today, you would probably describe her as a crusty old bird, a description she wouldn't be entirely displeased to hear. At an age when most of her peers have already retired and are taking life a little easy, Ellen is well into her third career, with every sign that she will be as successful as she has been in the past. But even as Ellen keeps up a pace that would wear out someone much younger, when you talk with her about education, she is likely to stop for a moment and even change her demeanor. "You know," she will say quietly, "education transformed my life in ways that I continue to discover every day. If it hadn't been for me completing my degree at 50-something [she is still coy about her age], I can't imagine where I would be today." To fully understand what she means, we will need to look at an earlier time in her life and when she was in partnership with a business tycoon.

Ellen grew up in a pre–World War II culture that didn't support women going to college unless they intended to become nurses or teachers. Ellen never wanted either: From as early as she could remember, she wanted to be involved with business at a level where she could exert some influence and make a difference. Her first venture involved working in a modest little florist shop. Because she was an extrovert, ambitious, young, and willing to work long hours, Ellen quickly began to get more actively involved in the business. She persuaded the owner, a kindly old man, to make some modest changes. Gradually, as more changes took place under Ellen's influence, the shop began attracting more customers and making more money than ever before. Still in her 20s, Ellen became a partner when the owner, Mr. Struzzo, indicated that he was ready to retire.

Ellen's second business began as a result of her continued success with the first. As Struzzo's Florist grew and flourished, Ellen gained more attention in the business community. Eventually, Arthur Mannikin, a successful local business tycoon and the owner of a professional baseball team, approached Ellen with a proposal to start a whole new business venture. Together, they created a service company relating to the travel industry that became nationally recognized, with Ellen overseeing the day-to-day operation and Mr. Mannikin handling the bigger details. For a few years, the business did wonderfully, but eventually the baseball team proved to be a serious problem. The team had a star who was the darling of fans everywhere, so when Mr. Mannikin suddenly traded him, the move was highly controversial and local fans were especially incensed. As a result, the business suffered critically and there was nothing Ellen could do to respond to the furor of the fans. Since she had sold her share of the florist shop to become partners with Mannikin, she now found herself in danger of losing everything and with no immediate viable options available to her. Despite her successful past, she found that because she lacked formal credentials, the only jobs available to her were at the entry level. She faced the option of retiring on a modest pension, but Ellen decided that she still had many things she wanted to accomplish and besides, she wanted to prove that the problems with the former business had nothing to do with her.

It was at this point in her life that she entered the Evening and Weekend College at Steinway University. As she said later, "I could see that having a degree would open many doors for me and besides, I had worked with lots of folks who already had their degrees and I knew I was smarter than them!" When the business closed down, Ellen took what money was left and committed it to completing her degree in business administration.

Steinway was a liberal arts school that required all students to complete a broad range of core courses. Although Ellen was initially only interested in the business courses, as she began taking courses in the humanities, social science, arts, and even math, she was pleasantly surprised and enthused about her education. Ellen was delighted to feel herself growing and becoming excited about many topics that she had never even considered before this time. She was particularly gratified to discover new interests and skills she never even realized she possessed. For instance, as a result of a project she had to do for a political science course, she became actively involved with local politics. (Today, she is a member of the school board.) When she took the required art history course, it helped her to feel more comfortable about her own creativity. (Now, she makes customized dolls for her friends and family.)

Today, Ellen is a district manager for an investment firm. She actually interned for the company while she was completing her degree. Although she thrives on the business elements of her job, she has learned to appreciate those moments when she and some of her younger staff have the opportunity to just talk about music or books or films that interest them. "Before I went to college, I never had the time or inclination for anything other than work. Today, this is my idea of 'stopping to smell the flowers' and I savor every moment of it!"

● ● ● ● ●

CONCLUSION

In 1994, I had the honor and pleasure to be a part of what was the final Lilly Endowment Workshop on the Liberal Arts. The Lilly Endowment had offered this workshop to colleges and universities for a number of years, but this was their last. This two-week session that brought 25 teams of faculty and administrators together in Colorado to work on various problems they were encountering on their campus proved to be one of the most stimulating and enlightening experiences of my life. Perhaps the workshop's central event—at least the activity that left the deepest impression on me—was an exercise in visioning the future. On its face value, this probably sounds like a rather trivial touchy-feely kind of exercise that ends with everyone forming a circle and singing "Kumbaya" around the campfire, but many of the participants have shared my belief that this was an important and perhaps even transforming moment in our careers.

Each person was asked to envision what his or her campus would look like in 20 years. The group spent an entire morning just on the envisioning portion of the exercise and later there were other activities that related to the various steps required to move from individual concept to more concrete forms of that vision before then articulating, with specific details, how the outcomes of your vision might look and feel. Eventually, everyone had the opportunity to share his or her vision with the entire group.

To my surprise in that exercise and subsequent sessions, I learned something about myself and my view of the future. I was surprised because I had never given the future enough time or energy to seriously consider what it might look like other than my assumption that it would probably resemble one step removed from what I was presently experiencing. But this exercise forced us all, I think, to see things differently. One of the things I learned was the high level of agreement that everyone shared concerning how technology would be increasingly important in higher education and that it would somehow transform the very nature of education. (To put this into perspective, less than 15% of the participants listed their email addresses in the directory at that time.) Now, less than halfway to that envisioned future, this aspect of the exercise seems to be proving itself correct. But that's where views of the future begin to dramatically diverge.

As I assembled the supportive materials for this chapter—possibly as a result of projecting how lifelong learning will impact the remainder of the century—I began to think about my experiences with the Lilly workshop. At that time, there was little, if any, consideration given to adult learners or the concept of lifelong learning—it would have been premature to think about then (even though it was less than ten years ago). But in a prescient moment, as part of his closing remarks to the entire workshop, David Smith (1994), one of the seminar leaders, made some important observations about the academy and its future. Although he never uses the term "lifelong learning," many of the central principles and practices that relate to the concept are clearly evident:

> The politics of the academy have never been more important than they are now, or will be in the foreseeable future. This was driven home to me by our futuring exercise as well as by seeing many team reports over the past few years. For the most part our campuses do not lack ideas, or even money. What we lack is the ability to get our act together and make those changes any social organism needs to make in a changing society. We don't need to do more work; we need to be willing to work differently.
>
> The core fact we must grasp is that communities beyond the faculty have a stake in the college's identity and mission. Colleges are dependent on the larger society, or parts thereof, in many ways: for students, for resources, as a destination for the college's human and intellectual products. That fact of interdependence mandates dialogue of a kind we do much too little of, and it requires responsiveness—neither subservience nor intransigence—on our part. (pp. 14–15)

I suppose that lifelong learning, as a way of life, will eventually be replaced by some other concept designed to better meet the needs of some future culture and society. But as I look in my crystal ball—and admittedly, it's somewhat cloudy—I believe lifelong learning will be at the very core of learning to work differently, growing interdependence, and responsive dialogue that must inevitably frame the 21st century. I can think of no more exciting time to be associated with higher education.

References

Bash, L., & Martyn, M. (2000). Building an empire by walking the dog: Revitalizing an adult program. *Proceedings of Alliance/ACE Conference, 20,* 21–27.

Cross, K. P. (1999). *Learning is about making connections.* Mission Viejo, CA: League for Innovation in the Community College.

Knox, A. B. (1990). Emerging imperatives for continuing professional education. *Visions for the Future of Continuing Professional Education.* Athens, GA: The University of Georgia.

Levine, A. E. (2000, October). The future of colleges: Nine inevitable changes. *The Chronicle of Higher Education,* pp. B10–B11.

Smith, D. H. (1994). *The college as a moral community.* Closing remarks presented at the Lilly Endowment Workshop on the Liberal Arts, Colorado Springs, CO.

Bibliography

Abeles, T. P. (2000). Caught in the rapids of change. *On the Horizon, 8* (6), 2–8.

Abeles, T. P. (2001). Partnering and cultural change. *On the Horizon, 9* (4), 2–3.

Allen, J. L., Miller, T. A., Fisher, B., & Moriarty, D. D. (1982). A survey of January interim psychology courses. *Teaching of Psychology, 9,* 230–231.

Altschuler, G. C., & McClure, P. (2002, January 18).... and colleges must create technology. *The Chronicle of Higher Education,* pp. B16–B17.

American Association of Retired Persons. (2000, July). *AARP survey on lifelong learning: Executive summary.* Retrieved April 6, 2002, from http://research.aarp.org/general/lifelong_1.html

American Council on Education & the Adult Higher Education Alliance. (1990). *Principles of good practice for alternative and external degree programs for adults.* Washington, DC: American Council on Education.

Apps, J. W. (1985). *Improving practice in continuing education: Modern approaches for understanding the field and determining priorities.* San Francisco, CA: Jossey-Bass.

Arden, E. (2001, April). Thinking about aged-based diversity. *AAHE Bulletin,* 7–8.

Arnold, T. (2002, Spring). Reliability and validity in assuring quality for prior learning assessment. *The Journal of Continuing Higher Education, 50* (2), 64–66.

Aslanian, C. (2001). *Adult students today.* Washington, DC: The College Board.

Astin, A. (1993). *What matters in college?* San Francisco, CA: Jossey-Bass.

Austin, T. L., Fennell, R. R., & Yeager, C. R. (1988). Class scheduling and academic achievement in a non-traditional graduate program. *Innovative Higher Education, 12,* 79–90.

Baden, C. (2002, Winter). The new entrepreneurship: What impact? *The Journal of Continuing Higher Education, 50* (1), 45–47.

Barber, B. R. (2002, Spring). The educated student: Global citizen or global consumer? *Liberal Education, 88* (2), 22–28.

Bash, L. (2000, February). *Bringing new meaning to the 'lifelong' of lifelong learning.* Paper presented at the meeting of the Association of Continuing Higher Education Region VI, Chicago, IL.

Bash, L. (2001, November). *Seeking new student profiles through alliances and underserved constituencies.* Paper presented at the meeting of the Council for Adult and Experiential Learning, Orlando, FL.

Bash, L. (2002, March). *Placing adult learners in 21st century perspective: Institutional models and lessons learned.* Paper presented at the meeting of the Higher Learning Commission (NCA) Conference, Chicago, IL.

Bash, L., Lighty, K., & Tebrock, D. (1999). Utilizing a "transformation" course to assist returning adult learners. *Proceedings of Alliance/ACE Conference, 19,* 1–5.

Bash, L., & Martyn, M. (2000). Building an empire by walking the dog: Revitalizing an adult program. *Proceedings of Alliance/ACE Conference, 20,* 21–27.

Bauer, D., & Mott, D. (1990). Life themes and motivations of re-entry students. *Journal of Counseling and Development, 68,* 555–560.

Baumgartner, L. M. (2001, Spring). An update on transformational learning. *New Directions for Adult and Continuing Education, 89,* 15–24.

Beck, R. A. (1979). Teaching statistics in an intensive semester program. *Improving College and University Teaching, 27,* 87–88.

Billington, D. D. (1996, May/June). Seven characteristics of highly effective adult learning programs. *New Horizons Electronic Journal.* Retrieved May 20, 2002, from http://www.newhorizons.org/article_billington1.html

Blumenstyk, G. (2002, June 28). Companies in the 'education industry' get optimistic revenue predictions. *The Chronicle of Higher Education,* p. A27.

Boddy, G. W. (1985). *Regular vs. compressed semester: A comparison of effectiveness for teaching in higher education.* Unpublished doctoral dissertation, University of Nebraska, Lincoln.

Bolman, L. G., & Deal, T. E. (1997). *Reframing organizations: Artistry, choice and leadership.* San Francisco, CA: Jossey-Bass.

Botkin, J. (1999). *Smart business: How knowledge communities can revolutionize your company.* New York, NY: The Free Press.

Braskamp, L. A., & Wergin, J. F. (1998). Forming new social partnerships. In W. G. Tierney (Ed.), *The responsive university: Restructuring for high performance* (pp. 62–91). Baltimore, MD: The Johns Hopkins University Press.

Breckon, D. J. (1989). Teaching college courses in compressed formats. *Lifelong Learning: An Omnibus of Practice and Research, 12* (4), 65–66.

Brendler, B., & Vonk, S. (2002, May). Creating a customer-centric culture through organizational assessment. Retrieved May 10, 2002, from http:/www.crm guru.com/features/2002b/0509bb.html

Brewer, P., & Sullivan, E. (2000). Defining good practice in adult degree programs. *NCA: A Collection of Papers on Self-study and Institutional Improvement,* 25–28.

Brookfield, S. D. (1986). *Understanding and facilitating adult learning.* San Francisco, CA: Jossey-Bass.

Brown, J. N. (1990). *Lifelong learning trends: A profile of continuing higher education.* Washington, DC: Publications Department, National University Continuing Education Association. (ERIC Document Reproduction Service No. ED319961)

Canja, E. T. (2002, Spring). Lifelong learning: Challenges & opportunities. *CAEL Forum and News,* 26–29.

Carlson, R. (1989, Spring). Malcolm Knowles: Apostle of andragogy. *Vitae Scholasticae, 8,* 1.

Carnevale, A. P. (2000). *Help wanted... college required.* Washington, DC: Educational Testing Service.

Centra, J. A., & Sobol, M. G. (1974). Faculty and student views of the interim term. *Research in Higher Education, 2,* 231–238.

Cervero, R. M., & Azzaretto, J. F. (Eds.). (1990). *Visions for the future of continuing professional education.* Athens, GA: University of Georgia Press.

Chaffee, E. E. (1998). Listening to the people we serve. In W. G. Tierney (Ed.), *The responsive university: Restructuring for high performance* (pp. 13–37). Baltimore, MD: The Johns Hopkins University Press.

Chickering, A., & Gamson, Z. (1987). Seven principles of good practice in undergraduate education. *AAHE Bulletin, 39,* 3–7.

Chickering, A. W., & Reisser, L. (1993). *Education and identity.* San Francisco, CA: Jossey-Bass.

Commission for a Nation of Lifelong Learners. (1997). *A nation learning: Vision for the 21st century.* Albany, NY: Regents College.

Commission on Higher Education and the Adult Learner. (1984). *Adult learners: Key to the nation's future.* Washington, DC: Author.

Commission on Non-Traditional Study. (1973). *Diversity by design.* San Francisco, CA: Jossey-Bass.

Council for Adult and Experiential Learning. (1999). *Serving adult learners in higher education.* Chicago, IL: Author.

Council for Adult and Experiential Learning. (2000a). *Principles of effectiveness for serving adult learners in higher education.* Chicago, IL: Author.

Council for Adult and Experiential Learning. (2000b). *Serving adult learners in higher education.* Chicago, IL: Author.

Council for Adult and Experiential Learning & the American Council on Education. (1993, March). *Adult degree programs: Quality issues, problem areas, and action steps.* Chicago, IL: Author.

Cranton, P. (2002, Spring). Teaching for transformation. *New Directions for Adult and Continuing Education, 93,* 63–71.

Cross, K. P. (1999). *Learning is about making connections.* Mission Viejo, CA: League for Innovation in the Community College.

Cross, K. P. (2001). Leading-edge efforts to improve teaching and learning. *Change, 33* (4), 31–37.

Crow, S. D. (2001, March). *Serving the common good: Consultant-evaluators in the heart of peer review.* Retrieved June 5, 2001, from http://www.ncahigher learningcommission.org/AnnualMeeting/archive/

Csikszentmihalyi, M. (1990). *Flow.* New York, NY: Harper & Row.

Csikszentmihalyi, M. (1996). Thoughts about education. In D. Dickinson (Ed.), *Creating the future: Perspectives on educational change.* Seattle, WA: New Horizons for Learning.

Deal, T. E. (1987). Building an effective organizational culture: How to be community-oriented in a traditional institution. In R. G. Simerly (Ed.), *Strategic planning and leadership in continuing education* (pp. 87–102), San Francisco, CA: Jossey-Bass.

deGroot, A. (1966). Perception and memory versus thought: Some old ideas and recent finds. In B. Kleinmuntz (Ed.), *Problem solving.* New York, NY: John Wiley.

DeZure, D. (Ed.) (2000). *Learning from change: Landmarks in teaching and learning in higher education from* Change *magazine 1969–1999.* Sterling, VA: Stylus.

Donaldson, J. F., & Graham, S. W. (2002, Spring). Accelerated degree programs: Design and policy implications. *The Journal of Continuing Higher Education, 50* (2), 2–13.

Doyle, R. J. (1978). *Intensive scheduling: The evidence for alternatives in course scheduling patterns.* Paper presented at the 18th Annual Forum of the Association for Industrial Research, Houston, TX.

Doyle, R. J., & Yantis, J. (1977). *Facilitating nontraditional learning: An update on research and evaluation in intensive scheduling.* Mount Pleasant, MI: Central Michigan University, Institute for Personal and Career Development. Eric Document Reproduction Service No. (ED144459)

Draves, W. A. (1997). *Learning in the 21st century* (2nd ed.). Manhattan, KS: Learning Resources Network.

Dychtwald, K., & Flower, J. (1989). *Age wave: The challenges and opportunities of an aging America.* Los Angeles, CA: Jeremy P. Tarcher, Inc.

Eddy, P. (2001, Fall). The story of Charlotte: An adult learner's view of higher education. *The Journal of Continuing Higher Education, 49* (3), 14–20.

Fischer, R. B., Blazey, M. L., & Lipman, H. T. (Eds.). (1992). *Students of the third age.* New York, NY: Macmillan.

Flint, T. A., & Associates (1999). *Best practices in adult learning: A CAEL/APQC benchmarking study.* New York, NY: Forbes Custom Publishing.

Freedman, L. (1987). *Quality in continuing education.* San Francisco, CA: Jossey-Bass.

Freire, P. (1970). *Pedagogy for the oppressed.* New York, NY: Seabury Press.

Fullan, M. (2001). *Leading in a culture of change.* San Francisco, CA: Jossey- Bass.

Fungaroli Sargent, C. (2000). *Traditional degrees for nontraditional students.* New York, NY: Farrar, Straus & Giroux.

Gardner, H., Csikszentmihalyi, M., & Damon, W. (2001). *Good work: When excellence and ethics meet.* New York, NY: Basic Books.

Gettinger, M. (1984). Individual differences in time needed for learning: A review of literature. *Educational Psychologist, 19* (1), 15–29.

Greenberg, D. (2001, July/August). The Trojan Horse of education. *On the Horizon, 9,* 4, 1, 4–5.

Gumport, P. J. (2001). A report to stakeholders on the condition and effectiveness of postsecondary education. *Change, 33* (3), 27–42.

Halfond, J. A. (2002, Spring). Further reflections on teaching. *The Journal of Continuing Higher Education, 50* (2), 50–52.

Hansman, C. A. (2001, Fall). The political landscape of adult education: From the personal to political and back again. *New Directions for Adult and Continuing Education, 91,* 85–93.

Hansman, C. A. (2001, Spring). Context-based adult learning. *New Directions for Adult and Continuing Education, 89,* 43–51.

Henry, G. T., & Basile, K. C. (1994). Understanding the decision to participate in formal adult education. *Adult Education Quarterly, 44* (2), 64–82.

Hermanson, K. (1996, November/December). Enhancing the effectiveness of adult learning programs: The importance of social and developmental learning. *New Horizons Electronic Journal.* Retrieved May 20, 2002, from http://www.newhorizons.org/article_hermansn.html

Herr, L. K. (2001, Winter). Survival in the new marketplace. *Assessment and Accountability Forum, 11* (4), 11-12, 18.

Horn, L. (1996). *Nontraditional undergraduates, trends in enrollment from 1986–1992 and persistence and attainment among 1989–90 beginning postsecondary students* (NCES 97–578). US Department of Education, NCES. Washington, DC: US Government Printing Office.

Houle, C. O. (1980). *Continuing learning in the professions.* San Francisco, CA: Jossey-Bass.

The Institute for Higher Education Policy. (1996). *Life after forty: A new portrait of today's—and tomorrow's—postsecondary students.* Boston, MA: The Education Resources Institute.

Johnson, D. W., Johnson, R. T., & Smith, K. A. (1998). *Active learning: Cooperation in the college classroom.* Edina, MN: Interaction Books.

King, K. P. (2002, Spring). Technology catalyzing change in how faculty teach and learn. *The Journal of Continuing Higher Education, 50* (2), 26–37.

Kipp, S. M. (1998). Demographic trends and their impact on the future of the Pell grant program. In L. E. Gladieux, B. Astor, & W. S. Swail (Eds.), *Memory, reason, and imagination: A quarter century of Pell grants* (p. 109). New York, NY: The College Board.

Kirby-Smith, J. P. (1987). *Effects of intensive college courses on student cognitive achievement, academic standards, student attitudes, and faculty attitudes.* Unpublished doctoral dissertation, University of Southern California, Los Angeles.

Knowles, M. S. (1975). *Self-directed learning: A guide for learners and teachers.* New York, NY: Cambridge Books.

Knowles, M. S. (1980). *The modern practice of adult education: From pedagogy to andragogy.* New York, NY: Cambridge Books.

Knowles, M. S. (1984). *Andragogy in action: Applying modern principles of adult learning.* San Francisco, CA: Jossey-Bass.

Knowles, M. S. (1990). Fostering competence in self-directed learning. In R. M. Smith (Ed.), *Learning to learn across the life span* (pp. 123–136). San Francisco: CA, Jossey-Bass.

Knox, A. B. (1990). Emerging imperatives for continuing professional education. *Visions for the Future of Continuing Professional Education.* Athens, GA: The University of Georgia.

Kolb, D. (1984). *Experiential learning: Experience as the source of learning and development.* Englewood Cliffs, NJ: Prentice-Hall.

Lamdin, L. (1997). *Earn college credit for what you know.* Dubuque, IA: Kendall/Hunt Publishing.

Lasker, H., Donnelly, J., & Weathersby, R. (1975). Even on Sunday: An approach to teaching intensive courses for adults. *Harvard Graduate School of Education Association Bulletin, 19,* 6–11.

The learning society: A report of the study on continuing education and the future. (1973). Notre Dame, IN: Center for Continuing Education, University of Notre Dame.

Leith, K. P. (1998, May). *Adult learning styles and critical thinking in psychology 100/101.* Paper presented at the meeting of the American Psychological Society Convention, Washington, DC.

Leskes, A. (2002, March). *Report of the Greater Expectations national panel* (draft Gex National Panel Report #7). Paper presented at the annual meeting of The Higher Learning Commission, Chicago, IL.

Levine, A. E. (2000, October). The future of colleges: Nine inevitable changes. *The Chronicle of Higher Education,* pp. B10–B11.

Levine, A., & Cureton, J. S. (1998). *When hope and fear collide: A portrait of today's college student.* San Francisco, CA: Jossey-Bass.

Lovett, C. M. (2002, March/April). Cracks in the bedrock: Can U.S. higher education remain number one? *Change,* 11–15.

Maclean, R. (2001, Winter). Notes and trends (forecasts for an aging society). *The Journal of Continuing Higher Education, 49* (1), 41–42.

Maehl, W. H. (2000). *Lifelong learning at its best: Innovative practices in adult credit programs.* San Francisco, CA: Jossey-Bass.

McBride, T. (2002, May 31). Curiously average: The way we teach. *The Chronicle of Higher Education,* p. B5.

Meister, J. C. (1994). *Corporate quality universities: Lessons in building a world-class work force.* Chicago, IL: Irwin Professional Publishing.

Merriam, S. B. (1988). *Case study research in education: A qualitative approach.* San Francisco, CA: Jossey-Bass.

Merriam, S. B. (2001a, Spring). Andragogy and self-directed learning: Pillars of adult learning theory. *New Directions for Adult and Continuing Education, 89,* 3–13.

Merriam, S. B. (2001b, Spring). Something old, something new: Adult learning theory for the twenty-first century. *New Directions for Adult and Continuing Education, 89,* 93–96.

Merriam, S. B., & Caffarella, R. S. (1991). *Learning in adulthood.* San Francisco, CA: Jossey-Bass.

Middle States Commission on Higher Education. (1996). *Assessing prior learning for credit.* Philadelphia, PA: Author.

Mims, S. K. (1983). The impact of time on art learning: Intensive vs. concurrent scheduling in higher education. *Studies in Art Education, 24* (2), 118–125.

Moe, M. T., & Blodget, H. (2000). *The knowledge web.* New York, NY: Merrill Lynch & Co.

Mortenson Research Seminar on Public Policy Analysis. (2001, November). *Postsecondary education opportunity.* Oskaloosa, IA: Author.

Mortenson Research Seminar on Public Policy Analysis. (2001, December). *Postsecondary education opportunity.* Oskaloosa, IA: Author.

National Center for Education Statistics. (1989). *Projections of education statistics to 2000.* Washington, DC: National Center for Education Statistics, Office of Educational Research and Improvement, US Department of Education.

Newman, F. (1999, March 5). *The transformation of American higher education.* Retrieved August 22, 2001, from http://www.futuresproject.org/publications/american_education.pdf

Newman, F. (1999, October 12). *Intellectual skills in the information age.* Retrieved August 22, 2001, from http://www.futuresproject.org/publications/intellectual_skills.pdf

Palmer Noone, L. (2000). Perceived barriers to innovation: First report from a study on innovation in higher education. *Assessment and Accountability Forum, 10* (2).

Pearson, C. S., Shavlik, D. L., & Touchton, J. G. (1989). *Educating the majority: Women challenge tradition in higher education.* New York, NY: American Council on Education & Macmillan Publishing Company.

Peters, J. M., Jarvis, P., & Associates (1991). *Adult education: Evolution and achievements in a developing field of study.* San Francisco, CA: Jossey- Bass.

Peterson, D. A. (1983). *Facilitating education for older learners.* San Francisco, CA: Jossey-Bass.

Pittman, V. (2002, Spring). Context v. content: An enduring battle in distance education. *The Journal of Continuing Higher Education, 50* (2), 59–60.

Queeney, D. S. (2001). The professionalization of continuing education. *The Journal of Continuing Higher Education, 49* (2), 43–44.

Ramaley, J., & Leskes, A. (2002, March). *Report of the Greater Expectations national panel.* Washington, DC: Association of American Colleges and Universities.

Ramaley, J., & Leskes, A. (2002, January). *Report of the Greater Expectations national panel.* Washington, DC: Association of American Colleges and Universities.

Ringel, R. L. (2000). Managing change in higher education. *Assessment and Accountability Forum, 10* (3).

Ross-Gordon, J. (2002, Spring). Effective teaching of adults: Themes and conclusions. *New Directions for Adult and Continuing Education, 93,* 85–91.

Sample, S. A. (2002). *The contrarian leader.* San Francisco, CA: Jossey-Bass.

Schlossberg, N. K., Lynch, A. Q., & Chickering, A. W. (1989). *Improving higher education environments for adults: Responsive programs and services from entry to departure.* San Francisco, CA: Jossey-Bass.

Schmidt, J. W. (1987). The leader's role in strategic planning. In R. G. Simerly (Ed.), *Strategic planning and leadership in continuing education* (pp. 31–50). San Francisco, CA: Jossey-Bass.

Schneider, C. G. (2001). Toward the engaged academy: New scholarship, new teaching. *Liberal Education,* 18–27.

Schneider, C. G. (2002, Winter/Spring). Can value added assessment raise the level of student accomplishment? *Peer Review,* 4–6.

Scott, P. A., & Conrad, C. F. (1992). A critique of intensive courses and an agenda for research. *Higher education: Handbook of theory and research.* New York, NY: The Association for Institutional Research and The Association for the Study of Higher Education.

Shapiro, N. S., & Levine, J. H. (1999). *Creating learning communities: A practical guide to winning support, organizing for change, and implementing programs.* San Francisco, CA: Jossey-Bass.

Sheared, V. (1994). Giving voice: A womanist construction. In E. Hayes & S. A. J. Colin III (Eds.), *Confronting racism and sexism in adult continuing education.* San Francisco, CA: Jossey-Bass.

Sheckley, B. G., & Weil, S. W. (1994). Using experience to enhance learning: Perspectives and questions. In M. T. Keeton (Ed.), *Perspectives on experiential learning: Prelude to a global conversation about learning* (pp. 7–12). Chicago, IL: Council for Adult Experiential Learning.

Shilling, K. M., & Shilling, K. (1999, May/June). Increasing expectations for student effort. *About Campus.*

Simerly, R. G., & Associates (1987). *Strategic planning and leadership in continuing education.* San Francisco, CA: Jossey-Bass.

Sissel, P. A., Hansman, C. A., & Kasworm, C. E. (2001, Fall). The politics of neglect: Adult learners in higher education. *New Directions for Adult and Continuing Education, 91,* 17–27.

Smith, B. L., & McCann, J. (Eds.) (2001). *Reinventing ourselves: Interdisciplinary education, collaborative learning, and experimentation in higher education,* Bolton, MA: Anker.

Smith, D. H. (1994). *The college as a moral community.* Closing remarks presented at the Lilly Endowment Workshop on the Liberal Arts, Colorado Springs, CO.

Smith, R. M., & Associates. (1990). *Learning to learn across the life span.* San Francisco, CA: Jossey-Bass.

Spence, L. D. (2001, December/January). The case against teaching. *Change,* 11–19.

Sperling, J. G. (2001, Fall). Vision of a visionary. *Assessment and Accountability Forum, 10* (3), 19–20.

Spratt, P. A. (1994). Needs and interests of adult learners: What do they seek on a campus? *NASPA Journal, 2* (4), 4–8.

Swail, W. S. (2002, July/August). Higher education and the new demographics: Questions for policy. *Change,* 15–23.

Task Force on Adult Degree Completion Programs. (2000, June). *Adult degree completion programs.* Retrieved June 5, 2001, from http://www.ncacihe.org/resources/adctf/ADCPRept.pdf

Taylor, M. C. (2001, December 14). Unplanned obsolescence and the new network culture. *The Chronicle of Higher Education,* pp. B14–B16.

Toffler, A. (1980). *The third wave.* New York, NY: Random House.

Tucker, R. W. (1997, Summer). The rhetoric of quality. *Assessment and Accountability Forum, 7* (2).

Tucker, R. W. (2001, Summer). A record year for adult-centered higher education. *Assessment and Accountability Forum, 11* (2), 3–9.

Tucker, R. W. (2001, Winter). Comment analysis and profiling: Decision support for management of academic quality. *Assessment and Accountability Forum, 11* (4), 3–7, 19.

Tucker, R. W., & Lamkin, R. (2001). Continuing education's new frontiers. *Assessment and Accountability, 11* (1), 11–18.

University Continuing Education Association. (2002). *Lifelong learning trends.* Washington, DC: Author.

University of Phoenix. (2000). *Yes, you can do this.* Retrieved June 12, 2002, from http://www.phoenix.edu

US Department of Education, National Center for Education Statistics. (2002). *The condition of education 2002* (NCES 2002-025). Washington, DC: Author.

van der Kamp, M., Slagter, M., & Hake, B. J. (2002, Winter). The role of higher education in lifelong learning: The Dutch case. *The Journal of Continuing Higher Education, 50,* (1), 37–44.

Vella, J. (2002, Spring). Quantum learning: Teaching as dialogue. *New Directions for Adult and Continuing Education, 93,* 73–83.

Votruba, J. C. (1987). From marginality to mainstream: Strategies for increasing internal support for continuing education. In R. G. Simerly & Associates (Eds.), *Strategic planning and leadership in continuing education* (pp. 185–201). San Francisco, CA: Jossey-Bass.

Walberg, H. J. (1988). Synthesis of research on time and learning. *Educational Leadership, 45* (6), 87–85.

Walshok, M. L. (1987). Developing a strategic marketing plan. In R. G Simerly (Ed.), *Strategic planning and leadership in continuing education* (pp. 149–167). San Francisco, CA: Jossey-Bass.

Watkins, B. T. (1989, November 1). Many colleges offering intensive weekend programs to give working adults a chance to earn degrees. *The Chronicle of Higher Education,* pp. A35, A38.

Watson, S. C. (2001). Institutional responses to adult students: Candid comments from students. *The Journal of Continuing Higher Education, 49* (2), 23–32.

Whitaker, U. (1989). *Assessing learning: Standards, principles & procedures.* Philadelphia, PA: Council for Adult and Experiential Learning.

Whitehead, A. N. (1929). *The aims of education and other essays.* New York, NY: Macmillan.

Widoff, J. C. (1999). The adult male undergraduate student experience: Real men do return to school. *The Journal of Continuing Higher Education, 47* (2), 15–24.

Young, J. R. (2001, December 14). MIT begins effort to create public web pages for more than 2,000 of its courses. *The Chronicle of Higher Education,* p. A34.

Young, J. R. (2002, May 31). The 24-hour professor. *The Chronicle of Higher Education,* pp. A31–A33.

Index